LIFE OF A MANSION

COOPER
HEWITT

Heather Ewing

LIFE OF A MANSION

THE STORY OF COOPER HEWITT, SMITHSONIAN DESIGN MUSEUM

CONTENTS

Endnotes are available online at cooperhewitt.org/life-of-mansion

Born decades apart and hailing from the United Kingdom, Andrew Carnegie and James Smithson shared a belief in innovation, education, transformative philanthropy, and risk taking. They both established institutions to promote the creation and diffusion of knowledge—Carnegie Corporation of New York and the Smithsonian Institution. Through their gifts to America, both changed this country forever, both for the good.

Although they never met, we meet them both through the works of skilled author and historian Heather Ewing. Her previous book, *The Lost World of James Smithson: Science, Revolution and the Birth of the Smithsonian*, is an insightful and enlightening account of why a man who never set foot on U.S. soil gave his entire fortune to a fledgling democracy. This new work, *Life of a Mansion: The Story of Cooper Hewitt, Smithsonian Design Museum*, published by Cooper Hewitt, is equally compelling. It tells the inspiring story of immigrant, industrialist, and innovator Andrew Carnegie through the lens of his Upper East Side Manhattan mansion. We discover how a youth who started as a bobbin boy in a textile mill worked hard, invested wisely, and became the richest man in the world, then threw himself into the task of giving it all away. The mansion, a technological marvel in its day, served as his home and office and was the birthplace of Carnegie Corporation of New York in 1911.

Thanks to a gift by Carnegie Corporation, the mansion is now home to Cooper Hewitt, Smithsonian Design Museum, the only museum in the country devoted exclusively to historic and contemporary design. It has served visitors from around the world since 1976, and its collection now holds more than 200,000 artifacts spanning thirty centuries, from all over the world. Its current reimagining features innovations Smithson and Carnegie would approve of, admire, and expect. Were they alive today, I think both would be surprised and delighted—as are we all. Enjoy!

*L*ife of a Mansion tells the story of the building Cooper Hewitt calls home. Andrew Carnegie's mansion was a technological marvel when it was completed in 1902, on a large block-long property facing Central Park. The neighborhood subsequently took his name, Carnegie Hill, reflecting his pioneering settlement of what he called "the highlands of Fifth Avenue." This book details how this grand and dynamic mansion has come to stand firmly as America's lens on design. Gluckman Mayner Architects and executive architect Beyer Blinder Belle undertook this most recent renovation together with the museum staff to modernize and make the most of Cooper Hewitt's spaces. Following three years of transformation inside and out, we've torn down walls metaphorically and physically.

Because this was a mammoth project—from the renovation of the entire Carnegie Mansion to the reinstallation of expanded exhibition galleries, including new case work throughout—we had the time to solidify a whole new direction and philosophy for the design museum experience. While our design resources and expertise become increasingly accessible worldwide, the mansion remains our anchor, the locus for life-changing programs for people of all ages.

The $91 million campaign to transform Cooper Hewitt was led by campaign committee co-chairs Harvey M. Krueger, Chairman Emeritus, and Michael R. Francis, trustee, along with trustees Paul Herzan, Barbara A. Mandel, Nancy Marks, Enid W. Morse, and Esme Usdan, and made possible with the major support of the Smithsonian, the museum's dedicated board of trustees, New York City, and many corporations, foundations, and individuals. Numerous spaces throughout the museum were named in recognition of donors' generosity, as you'll see throughout these pages and in the galleries.

There are many people to thank for the creation of this important book. First and foremost, sincere thanks to Heather Ewing, author and architectural historian, who wrote this exciting publication after countless hours of research. Thanks also to Pamela Horn, Cooper Hewitt's Head of Cross-Platform Publishing, who worked tirelessly on this and additional major titles in preparation for the museum's opening. Special thanks also to Susan Henshaw Jones, the Ronay Menschel Director of the Museum of the City of New York, and her staff, for providing the original 1938 images of the Carnegie Mansion, which were so essential to the success of this book. We also appreciate the funding provided by the museum's Andrew W. Mellon Foundation Publications Fund and by Furthermore: a program of the J. M. Kaplan Fund.

COOPER HEWITT

7

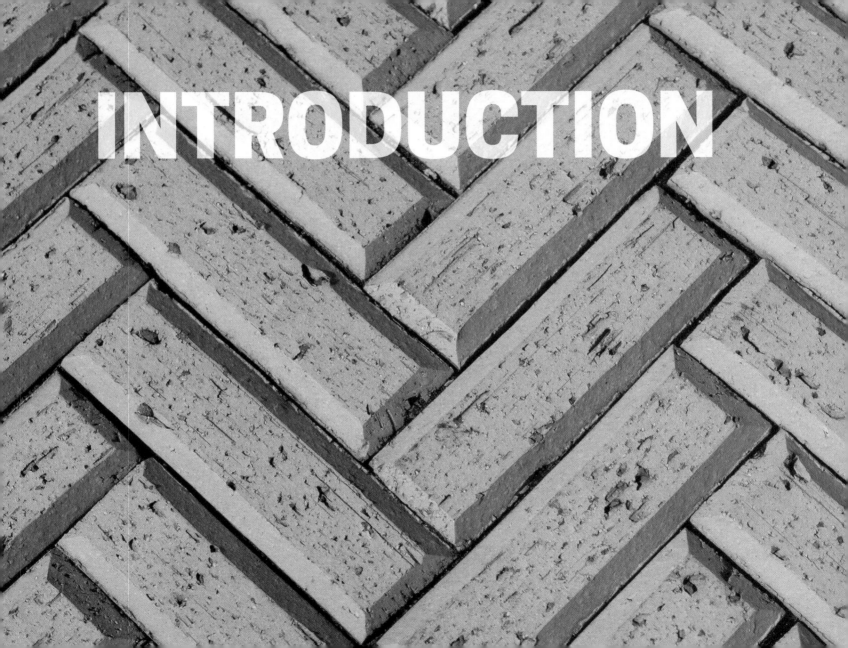

INTRODUCTION

On the morning of December 12, 1902, a horse and carriage carrying the Carnegie family—Andrew, Louise, and five-year-old Margaret—arrived at the front door of 2 East 91st Street for the first time. The family had come direct from the *Oceanic*, the liner that had carried them on a rough and wintry passage from their Scotland home, Skibo Castle, after a six-month European sojourn.

To the crowd waiting at the pier in New York, Andrew Carnegie seemed frail and much aged. He leaned on Mrs. Carnegie's arm as they exited the ship; his physician, who had crossed with them, stayed nearby. But he had lost none of his sparkle or wit. "Why, I am fit as a brand new piston rod and solid as a rock!" he reassured the waiting journalists with a laugh. New York was blanketed in snow, and the horses trundled them through Central Park up to the Tiffany-style entrance porch of their new home. There Andrew Carnegie turned and presented his beloved little daughter with the key to the brand-new mansion.

Inside, all the servants were lined up in the hall to welcome the family. Walter C. Gale, the organist at the Broadway Tabernacle, was playing the organ. The house was completely furnished, the pictures hung on the walls, and the lights all ablaze. In the rear, giant full-size trees had been transplanted from the woods of Connecticut and New York State, so the spacious garden appeared as if it had been there for decades. Howard Russell Butler, the artist-impresario who had overseen the mansion's construction and outfitting, was on hand to tour the family through the rooms. Carnegie was "very pleased with the house," his wife reported in her diary that evening—evidently with some relief, as it was Louise who had been largely responsible for the design decisions over the previous four years.

Carnegie arrived back in the United States raring to go. "The voyage has restored me and I am ready for work of which I find plenty," he wrote a friend. "Bertram [James Bertram, Carnegie's secretary] tells me four hundred American applications for Libraries in, also 260 from other parts of the E.[nglish] S.[speaking] Race so I have 660 to deal with. The field is not yet filled as you see."

Carnegie's work lay now in giving away the hundreds of millions that he had amassed in the previous decades. Just the year before, in 1901, he had finally sold Carnegie Steel to J. P. Morgan, creating U.S. Steel, the nation's first billion-dollar company, and making Carnegie in the process arguably the richest man in the world. He would remain so for the next decade, displaced only by the forced liquidation of Standard Oil in 1913, which vaulted John D. Rockefeller to the top. The house at 2 East 91st Street was to be the primary headquarters from which this philanthropy would emanate, and it was also the birthplace of Carnegie Corporation of New York, the foundation Carnegie created in 1911 to distribute funds on a larger scale and to continue this work after his death, once he realized that he would need several more lifetimes to give away all that he had accumulated.

It was, above all, to be a home—a place Carnegie had long yearned for, without even realizing it. (For the two

OPPOSITE Detail of the yellow brick paving at the entrance to the mansion.

The entrance to the Carnegie Mansion at 2 East 91st Street.

The Carnegie Mansion from Fifth Avenue.

decades that Carnegie lived in New York City prior to his marriage at age fifty-one, his residence was a hotel suite that he shared with his mother.) Family was now his first priority, even as Carnegie took his place on the world stage, endowing libraries and institutions for the promotion of knowledge, writing books, and lobbying for world peace (work that included the creation of the Carnegie Hero Fund, with separate endowments in ten other countries; and the establishment of the Peace Palace in The Hague, Netherlands, the Pan American Union in Washington, D.C., and a Central American Court of Justice in Cartago, Costa Rica).

Carnegie enjoyed nearly two decades in this mansion before his death in 1919 (unlike his former partner Henry Clay Frick, who lived five years in his beautiful Fifth Avenue palace, today the Frick Collection; or the railroad titan E. H. Harriman, who lived only five weeks in Arden House, his gargantuan estate on a mountaintop in Harriman, New York, some forty miles outside New York City). His wife, Louise, remained in the house, carrying on many of the traditions, entertaining her grandchildren, and holding organ concerts, occasional benefits, and other events, until her death in 1946.

After the family was gone, the Carnegie Mansion found new life as a school. For two decades it served as the headquarters of the Columbia University School of Social Work. Then, in 1972, Carnegie Corporation donated the mansion to the Smithsonian Institution. Restored and adapted for use as a museum, it opened to the public in 1976 as Cooper-Hewitt, the Smithsonian's first museum outside of Washington, D.C. The museum's foundational collection had been formed in the late nineteenth century by the Hewitt sisters, three women who had known Andrew Carnegie and whose grandfather, industrialist and philanthropist Peter Cooper, had been one of Carnegie's great role models and inspirations. Dedicated to educating, inspiring, and empowering people through design, Cooper Hewitt, Smithsonian Design Museum has found a fitting home in the mansion of a man who throughout his life embraced innovation and learning.

A portrait of Louise and Margaret Carnegie painted at the mansion in 1903 soon after the family had moved in, by the Scottish artist and friend of Andrew Carnegie, Alexander Roche.

ANDREW CARNEGIE

Andrew Carnegie was born in Scotland in 1835, in a one-room cottage in the town of Dunfermline, which for more than a hundred years had been a center for designing and producing fine damask linen. His father was a handloom weaver, "one of the most lovable of men," according to Andrew, but "not much a man of the world." In the mid-nineteenth century, the power, or steam, loom and the Industrial Revolution it represented displaced the father, though they would one day make the son the richest man in the world. The family emigrated to the United States in 1848, when Carnegie was twelve, and they settled in the environs of Pittsburgh. His mother, Margaret, was the family's mainstay and soon became the primary breadwinner; Carnegie idolized her all his life (and could not bring himself to marry until after her death).

Carnegie began his working life as a bobbin boy in a textile mill but soon managed to get a job as a telegraph messenger boy. From working in a cellar running a steam engine, "begrimed with coal dirt," he felt he was "lifted into paradise . . . with newspapers, pens, pencils, and sunshine about me—I felt that my foot was upon the ladder and that I was bound to climb." And so he did—he was soon promoted to telegraph operator and then to personal assistant to the regional head of the Pennsylvania Railroad. He began making his first investments—in sleeping cars and oil and iron. Within a few years of the end of the Civil War, he had achieved an annual income in dividends of more than $50,000.

Andrew at age sixteen with his younger brother, Tom, 1851.
BACKGROUND The Carnegie tartan.

NIGHT VIEW OF CARNEGIE ILLINOIS STEEL MILL ON MONONGAHELA RIVER, CLAIRTON WORKS

CL.400

At this time iron was the metal used in most manufactures, as steel could be produced only in small quantities. Carnegie was one of the first to capitalize on the English inventor Henry Bessemer's new process to convert molten iron into molten steel. For the coke (made from coal) needed for the process, he formed a relationship with Henry Clay Frick, enabling Carnegie to vertically integrate the entire steelmaking process. Carnegie's subsequent steelworks fueled the expansion of the country—its bridges, railroads, structural steel, and armor plate—and created the wealth that led to Carnegie's ultimate legacy, his philanthropy.

ABOVE LEFT Andrew Carnegie's birthplace in Dunfermline, Scotland.
ABOVE RIGHT Andrew Carnegie, 1913.
RIGHT The Carnegie steelworks in Pittsburgh, source of Carnegie's fortune.

THE BIRTH OF A CHILD

In 1897, at the age of sixty-one, Andrew Carnegie became a father. He was ten years into his marriage, and his wife had just turned forty. Their daughter, Margaret, became the center of their world; she was, in the eyes of her father, "fresh from heaven," and he called her "the Little Saint."

Carnegie had not yet retired, despite having vowed when he was young that he would step down from money-making at age thirty-five in order to pursue an education and self-improvement, while spending "the surplus [of his income] each year for benevolent purposes." Carnegie Steel was thriving—"Our organization was never so perfect," Carnegie said—and was making more money than ever. It was producing half the country's structural steel. The thrill of competition, the opportunity to increase both profitability and market share, proved irresistible, and Carnegie doubled down on his investments. Net profits rose from $7 million in 1897 to $16 million a year later. In 1899 they went still higher, to $21 million, and he and Frick anticipated $40 million by 1900.

The family was then living in an elegant Second Empire–style town house near the corner of Fifth Avenue and 51st Street. It had been one of Andrew's wedding gifts to his wife (the other was an annual income of $20,000—the equivalent of about half a million dollars today). Carnegie was perfectly happy to remain at that address: "The sewage system was imperfect, and the kitchen, pantry, and conservatory needed attention," but

OPPOSITE Detail of the decorative plasterwork in the reception room ceiling.

Louise and baby Margaret at the Carnegie home on West 51st Street, 1897.

it was nothing that couldn't be fixed, and Carnegie hired Howard Russell Butler, the artist-lawyer whom he had appointed manager of the concert venue Carnegie Hall, to supervise the renovation work over the summer of 1897.

HOWARD RUSSELL BUTLER

Howard Russell Butler in his studio in Princeton, New Jersey, ca. 1920.

Howard Russell Butler (1856–1934) was a lawyer turned artist, the greater part of whose working career revolved around Andrew Carnegie. After graduating from Princeton, he accompanied the Princeton Scientific Expedition to the Rocky Mountains and then began his career working for Western Union, making illustrations of the electric telegraph, Thomas Alva Edison's inventions, and other innovations. He attended Columbia Law School, was accepted to the bar, and practiced for three years before leaving to embark on a career in the arts. At age twenty-eight he went to Mexico to study with the well-known landscape painter Frederic Edwin Church, and he subsequently studied in Paris. In 1889, he settled in New York. As an artist with a flair for business, he soon became a leading force for the creation of a new umbrella organization for artists' and architects' groups, with the idea of providing a central building with office and exhibition space.

Butler's American Fine Arts Society proved hugely popular among New York artists and architects. To fund the construction of a new building, however, Butler needed large ($5,000) subscriptions from patrons. His first patron, according to his diary, was George W. Vanderbilt (builder of Biltmore House in Asheville, North Carolina, then the largest house in the United States). As he sought out others, he "naturally thought of Andrew Carnegie." Conveniently, Butler's father had recently been on a steamer crossing the Atlantic with

I saw both sides of his character. I benefited by his highminded and generous qualities, and suffered under his meanness. In his library, which was really his New York office, in many long walks through streets and in Central Park; at Cluny, Skibo, and Cannes; on his yacht on the Mediterranean; on golf courses; at the sittings for portraits . . . on all of these occasions we were thrown so closely together, and discussed so many themes and current topics, that I almost came to believe that I could look into his inmost soul. And yet I never did. He remained to me an enigma to the end.
— Howard Russell Butler on Andrew Carnegie

Carnegie and was able to provide his son with a letter of introduction.

The encounter, which Butler described at length in his diary, is a charming one—and reveals something of the playful and engaging way in which Andrew Carnegie approached philanthropy. Over several meetings, Carnegie told Butler repeatedly that he wouldn't give him a cent. But Butler was persistent, and eventually Carnegie gave him five bonds of H. C. Frick Coke Company. Sometime later, Butler called on Carnegie and announced that he had five coke bonds to sell. "I met Mr. Carnegie's wink and twinkle with a smile as I walked out," he wrote in his diary. Ultimately, Carnegie became head of the board of trustees of the American Fine Arts Society. (The building still exists today, on West 57th Street, housing one of the original member groups, the Art Students League of New York.)

COOPER HEWITT

Carnegie Hall in 1899. Andrew and Louise Carnegie met the conductor Walter Damrosch on board the ship they took to Europe on their honeymoon. From the friendship that ensued came the idea for a new Carnegie-backed music hall for New York. It opened to the public in 1891, with guest of honor Pyotr Ilyich Tchaikovsky conducting. By 1894, the hall's original, plain name, "Music Hall," was replaced with Carnegie Hall. Howard Russell Butler served as president of Carnegie Hall from 1896 to 1905.

Impressed with Butler, Carnegie made him director of operations at Carnegie Hall and then hired him as well to be one of his personal attorneys. It was Butler who bought the Upper East Side lots that eventually comprised the Carnegie Mansion property, protecting Carnegie from owners who might inflate their prices for such a wealthy buyer. He served as liaison between the Carnegies and the architects, developing the original program and architectural footprint of the building, managing the competition, and coordinating the house's interior design. He also became something of an official Carnegie portraitist, painting at least thirteen pictures of Andrew, many of which were placed in Carnegie libraries and other benefactions, as well as several posthumous portraits of Andrew Carnegie's mother.

The year the Carnegies settled in their new mansion, Butler and his family moved into one of the adjacent properties, a house at 22 East 91st Street (which they rented from Carnegie). As work on the mansion came to a close, Butler introduced Carnegie to the idea of funding a new lake at Princeton, for the use of the university's rowing team. The creation of Carnegie Lake did not prove easy, however, and ended up costing much more than envisioned. It ultimately also cost Butler his relationship with Carnegie, who told the artist it was "the worst thing" with which he was ever involved.

Long Island Landscape, a painting by Howard Russell Butler installed over the dining room mantel in the Carnegie Mansion.

Each year Mrs. Carnegie chose one of her color autochrome photographs of the Skibo grounds for the family's Christmas card.

Louise Carnegie, however, had her heart set on a completely new house, built from scratch. Even when Andrew Carnegie shifted gears, from some renovation work to total reconstruction, bottom to top, on the West 51st Street property—asking Butler to prepare plans using the New York architect Henry J. Hardenbergh—Louise held her ground. Butler traveled all the way to Cannes, France, where the Carnegies were wintering with their new infant, to present them with the plans, and Louise rejected them

out of hand. She and Butler then sat down and started sketching ideas for a brand-new property. It was the beginning of a fruitful collaboration.

Margaret's arrival changed many things. Since the Carnegies' marriage, they had made a tradition of spending the summers in Carnegie's native Scotland. For a decade they rented Cluny Castle in the central Highlands. But, as Louise wrote to her husband, "We now want to take root . . . a home first, please." Unable to purchase Cluny from its ancestral owners, Carnegie settled on Skibo Castle, a medieval castle on 20,000 acres in the Highlands near Dornoch. Just as the family was beginning to think of a new home in New York City, they also embarked on a massive building campaign at Skibo, hiring local Inverness-based architects Ross & Macbeth to update and enlarge the house.

Mrs. Carnegie's first criterion for her new New York City home was that it occupy "a square of four city lots." (In the end it actually took up eleven lots, and the garden occupied another nine.) She wanted extensive open space and greenery for her child. Fashionable New York in the 1890s was centered on Fifth Avenue in the Fifties, anchored around the Vanderbilt mansion at 52nd Street (one block north of where the Carnegies were then living). Society continued to creep northward up the island, as it had done for decades, but the Seventies were then pretty much the limit. The Carnegies chose a spot more than a mile farther north—an area that was remote, rural, and

SKIBO CASTLE: THE CARNEGIE STYLE

Louise called Skibo "a fairyland of childhood," and much of the planning revolved around creating an ideal home for their child. (Margaret, in fact, at age two, laid the cornerstone for the new construction.) In Europe Carnegie felt a little freer to pursue a more grandiose and extravagant lifestyle. The new construction included a new wing to the north with a huge modern kitchen and quarters for the servants, and on the southwest, with views over the estate, a suite of new rooms: drawing room, music room, and Carnegie's library. As would be the case in New York, it was Louise who worked most closely with the architects. Many of the traditions of their New York life, as well as their taste in furnishing and interior decoration, were first established in Scotland. At its height, Skibo had eighty-five domestic staff, eighteen gardeners, an organist, a piper, and a gamekeeper.

The library was paneled with Scottish oak and held 7,000 volumes. Encircling the room were the coats of arms of all the Scottish towns that had given Carnegie a key to their city.

The Carnegies built a spectacular enclosed pool, with Turkish baths.

Skibo remained in the family until 1982, when Margaret (who lived until 1990) finally sold it. It became the Carnegie Club, a private membership sporting estate. Some aspects of the Carnegie lifestyle still remain today: the organ in the front hall is regularly played, and a bagpiper serenades the castle each morning.

The main hall featured, in addition to the organ, a stained-glass window that Carnegie loved to show to guests. It depicted both the boat that he rode in steerage on to the United States as a boy in 1848 and the luxurious "floating palace" on which he returned in triumph to his homeland.

distinctly unglamorous. "It was, in a word," one magazine article wrote, "only one remove from goatville." The site was occupied by a riding academy and surrounded by a lemonade stand and a series of shanty-like houses. Farther east were rows of middle-class town houses, developed in connection with the Second Avenue elevated subway.

Using Butler and one other as his proxies, Carnegie successfully engineered the purchase, virtually overnight, of the lots he had targeted for his mansion, as well as many of the lots in the block north of his house, between 91st and 92nd Streets—including all of those facing Fifth Avenue and Central Park.

Butler then worked closely with the Carnegies to determine their needs—Carnegie was adamant that there be no ballroom in any house of his, for example—before developing the floor plans. He spent six weeks in early 1899 drawing up the plans for the two principal floors, with the size and arrangement of the rooms "pretty well thought out." As soon as they were complete, he organized an architectural competition. Butler proposed five local firms, which Carnegie narrowed to three: Henry J. Hardenbergh, architect of the Dakota apartment building and the Waldorf-Astoria hotel; Howard, Cauldwell & Morgan, whose principal John Galen Howard soon after went on to design the campus of University of California at Berkeley; and Babb, Cook & Willard.

The architects to whom Carnegie wrote to invite them to design his house were not the top tier then dominating

Carnegie and his friend Henry Pritchett, the former president of the Massachusetts Institute of Technology, who became the first president of the Carnegie Foundation for the Advancement of Teaching, walking near Central Park, 1908.

the construction of Gilded Age mansions—McKim, Mead & White, and Carrère and Hastings held that position—but they seem to have been people that Butler knew personally and felt comfortable working with. Butler knew Hardenbergh well from the days of the American Fine Arts

OPPOSITE Shanties in the vicinity of Fifth Avenue and 90th Street, ca. 1880.

Babb, Cook & Willard's competition drawings were first unveiled to the public in the *Architectural Record* of July 1899. The architects modified the plans after they won the competition; this north elevation shows the east end of the building, where the picture gallery was to be, as several stories in height, rather than the single story it became.

Society, for example, when Butler was president and Hardenbergh secretary. In fact, Babb, Cook & Willard had been finalists in the competition to design the American Fine Arts Society building. These firms were also chosen, as Carnegie informed them, because they were the only architects in the city who had not begged for the job.

Carnegie had requested "a plain home, roomy and comfortable . . . the most modest and roomy house in New York." From Butler's program and plans, the three firms came up with very different solutions. William T. Partridge, then a young architect working for Howard, Cauldwell & Morgan, recalled in his memoirs that his firm and Hardenbergh's had both scoffed at Butler's directives and ignored them in their competition entries. Howard, he said, was convinced that after a few years in New York, Carnegie's social status would "defeat his desire for domesticity," so he opted for magnificence in his proposal. Hardenbergh proposed a French Renaissance chateau-style design for Carnegie's property, which would have represented the height of Gilded Age extravagance; Howard, Cauldwell & Morgan submitted a Colonial-style design. Babb, Cook & Willard, who followed the plans most closely, submitted a Georgian-style building, and it was their design that was accepted.

The house was a massive four-story block, running some 175 feet in length, atop a substantial rusticated limestone base. Georgian Revival in style, with strong Beaux Arts elements, the building was faced with Flemish-bond brickwork and featured heavy limestone quoining and trim around the windows. Above a dentilled cornice sat a stone parapet with decorative urns.

Unusually, the house was positioned right up along the northern end of the block facing 91st Street, leaving the majority of the property open for the garden. The architect Walter Cook noted at the time, "It is a somewhat remarkable thing that until Mr. Carnegie came to build his house not one of the owners of great fortunes in New York seemed to have thought of a garden space around their dwellings as a legitimate expenditure, giving pleasure to themselves and the public, and adding greatly to the beauty and pleasure of their dwelling."

According to Butler, Carnegie "had little idea of the requirements of architectural design." He had chosen the Georgian-style entry, which called for symmetry, but he wanted flexibility—and he periodically requested changes in window positions and sizes and put forward other whims. It did not make for easy architect-client relations. The last straw for the architect was Carnegie's request that the stone arch and steps that led from the reception room to the terrace on the south side of the mansion be replaced with a rustic bridge. "It was inevitable that Mr. Cook and Mr. Carnegie could not get on together. Carnegie's comments to me about Cook are omitted [from this diary]," Butler wrote. "It was good that there was a go-between."

UPPER EAST SIDE, 1911

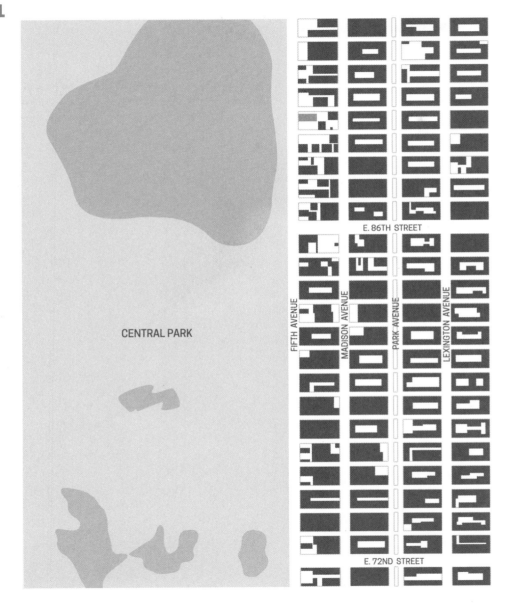

CENTRAL PARK

E. 86TH STREET

E. 72ND STREET

FIFTH AVENUE

MADISON AVENUE

PARK AVENUE

LEXINGTON AVENUE

 1911

CARNEGIE-OCCUPIED BUILDINGS

LOTS PURCHASED BY CARNEGIE

CARNEGIE HILL, 1911
CARNEGIE'S PROPERTIES, 1898–1920

CENTRAL PARK

E. 92ND STREET

E. 91ST STREET

MANSION (1902)

MILLER HOUSE
(FROM 1920)

GARAGE
(1905)

E. 90TH STREET

E. 89TH STREET

E. 88TH STREET

FIFTH AVENUE

MADISON AVENUE

PARK AVENUE

THE HIGHLANDS OF FIFTH AVENUE

The area that Carnegie selected to build his house was the highest point along Fifth Avenue. It was originally called Prospect Hill, but Carnegie referred to it fondly as "the highlands of Fifth Avenue." When the news of Carnegie's land purchases hit the papers, it caused a sensation. A rush of real estate speculation followed. Because of the development spurred by his arrival, the area soon became known as Carnegie Hill.

Although Carnegie settled far to the north of established society in choosing his home on East 91st Street, he did not intend to leave the selection of his neighbors to chance. In purchasing most of the surrounding property, Carnegie sought to sell lots to people who would make congenial neighbors and put up elegant mansions.

One of the earliest purchasers was William D. Sloane, of the furniture company W. & J. Sloane, who acquired two lots from Carnegie in 1902, numbers 7 and 9 East 91st Street, and had houses built as gifts for his newly married daughters. Emily Vanderbilt Sloane and her husband, banker John Henry Hammond, received a magnificent Carrère and Hastings–designed, Renaissance-style, limestone-faced palazzo at 9 East 91st Street. Florence Adele Sloane and her husband, James A. Burden Jr., enjoyed an exquisite Beaux Arts–style town house by Warren and Wetmore, the firm that later designed Grand Central Terminal.

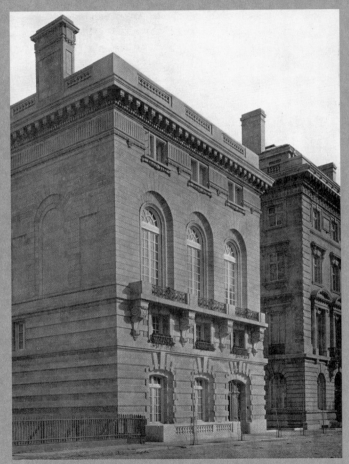

Numbers 7 and 9 East 91st Street, across from the Carnegie Mansion, in 1907.

James Burden's uncle I. Townsend Burden was another of the earliest buyers, acquiring the lot at the corner of Fifth Avenue and 92nd Street in 1902, where he built an enormous five-story redbrick and limestone house designed by Philadelphia architect Horace Trumbauer. The Burdens were Carnegie's ideal neighbor: the family was of Scots ancestry and had made their fortune in ironworks. The house, which was later occupied by Marjorie Merriweather Post and her second husband, E. F. Hutton, was replaced by an apartment building in 1924.

Fifth Avenue and East 91st Street in 1911, showing the Carnegie Mansion and the Hammond and Burden Houses, published in *Fifth Avenue, New York, from Start to Finish* (New York: Welles & Co., 1911), a kind of Gilded Age Google Street View of New York's most fashionable thoroughfare.

Otto Kahn's mansion at 1 East 91st Street, built by J. Armstrong Stenhouse and C. P. H. Gilbert, was modeled after the Palazzo della Cancelleria in Rome. A magnificent eighty-room Italian Renaissance–style mansion, it was completed in 1918 and featured a private courtyard entrance. In 1934 the mansion became home to the Convent of the Sacred Heart, which still owns it today along with the adjacent number 7 East 91st Street.

William Sloane's mother, Euphemia, had been a childhood friend of Andrew Carnegie's mother in Scotland, and his father and Carnegie's father had been fellow weavers. The Sloanes were the first people Carnegie's family connected with upon their arrival in the United States. As Carnegie wrote in his autobiography, "It was a genuine pleasure when Willie . . . bought ground from me in 1900 opposite our New York residence for his two married daughters so that our children of the third generation became playmates as our mothers were in Scotland."

Some of Carnegie's lots remained undeveloped for a number of years. Carnegie sold the corner lot across 91st Street in 1913 to investment banker Otto Kahn. Kahn paid nearly as much for that one lot as Carnegie had paid for all the properties he bought in 1898—a testament to the impact that Carnegie had on the real estate development of Carnegie Hill.

For nearly all the years that Carnegie lived at 2 East 91st Street, the property to the south of the garden looked as it had since "time almost immemorial," according to the *New York Times*. An old wooden shack stood at the corner, dispensing "pink lemonade, peanuts, bananas, huge ginger cakes, and other delicacies." Carnegie only finally purchased the property in 1917, when it seemed likely an apartment building might go up that would overshadow their beloved garden.

THE ARCHITECTS: BABB, COOK & WILLARD

At the time that Babb, Cook & Willard began work on the Carnegie Mansion, they were best known for their New York Life Insurance building in Montreal, then the tallest building in the province of Quebec. They had also, early in their career, made a mark in downtown New York with the robust Romanesque Revival–style Devinne Press Building on Lafayette Street. One can imagine Carnegie feeling comfortable around architects who excelled in using the latest engineering and technology, but he was probably also drawn to Babb, Cook & Willard's residential work; in the late 1890s they were in the process of designing two houses for Frederic B. Pratt, whose father had founded the Pratt Institute— a large house with a garden in Brooklyn and a country house in Glen Cove on the North Shore of Long Island.

George Fletcher Babb was the oldest of the partners, virtually the same age as Andrew Carnegie. Early in his career Babb had been a senior designer in the office of the renowned neo-Gothic architect and writer Russell Sturgis, where he became close with fellow architects William R. Mead and Charles Follen McKim. It was through McKim, in fact, that Babb met his future partner Walter Cook.

Walter Cook went from Harvard to postgraduate studies at the Polytechnic in Munich and the École des Beaux-Arts in Paris (where he briefly overlapped with McKim). From Europe he went straight into a partnership with Babb in 1877. Why Babb took as his partner a young tyro with no experience in an architectural office was simple: Cook brought the assurance of work. In fact, the first project the new firm did was for Cook's mother.

Babb and Cook worked together for seven years before they took on Daniel W. Willard. Willard had trained as an engineer at the Massachusetts Institute of Technology; his first job out of college was as the principal of an evening school focused on industrial technical education, but he left that position for several years to head west with a former classmate to raise sheep in the Wyoming Territory. Back in New York he worked for architect H. J. Hardenbergh (one of the competitors for the Carnegie Mansion commission) and became the first president of the newly founded Architectural League of New York in 1881. Willard's presence enabled the firm to tackle more complicated buildings, notably the Devinne Press Building, which featured heavy interior masonry arches to support the weight of the printing presses. By the mid-1890s, however, the West beckoned once more, and Willard moved to California, to settle in Redlands. He had an interesting later career, creating some theater designs and acquiring a few patents for his inventions, including his contribution to the Allied cause during World War I, a net for the purpose of entangling submarines.

The Devinne Press Building of 1886, one of the most sophisticated masonry buildings of its time, remains one of New York City's architectural masterpieces.

The firm carried on for several years more as Babb, Cook & Willard. Although Willard's name was still on the masthead at the time of the Carnegie commission, he was not involved in the design of the mansion and likely no longer active in the firm. In 1898, Babb and Cook joined forces with W. A. Welch, but it was another decade before Babb, Cook & Willard was formally dissolved and a new partnership, Babb, Cook & Welch, was formed.

The firm was in their day considered "leaders of the profession in the East." By the turn of the century, however, when they won the Carnegie Mansion project, they were not so in fashion. Babb's position in particular had declined, and although he was still close with sculptor Augustus Saint-Gaudens, he had lost many of his social contacts. Architect Stanford White of McKim, Mead & White told Saint-Gaudens in 1905 that Babb neglected himself so much that any room he entered had to be fumigated after he left. The Carnegies were probably spared Babb's hygiene issues, however, as it was Walter Cook (making the most of his Scots ancestry) who interacted with the family. Cook went on to serve on the advisory committee that oversaw the design of the Carnegie branch libraries for New York City.

The Frederic B. Pratt House in Brooklyn (today the home of the president of Pratt Institute and called the Caroline Ladd Pratt House) may have been something of a model for the Carnegies.

In the original plans for the house, the architects designed a massive stone terrace running the full length of the house. This feature, with its tremendous granite base and limestone balustrade, was nearly completed when Carnegie suddenly ordered the terrace removed—claiming that he'd had no idea that it was going to be so large or long. He wanted flower beds under the window of his office, not an imposing stone terrace. This reversal was, understandably, greatly distressing to the architects, but the ever-tactful Howard Russell Butler managed to find a solution by lopping off one large section of the west end of the terrace and terminating it with a flight of steps.

RIGHT Andrew Carnegie on the terrace, soon after the completion of the house.
OPPOSITE The house with its stone terrace, c. 1902.

THE MANSION AS HOME

Within a few weeks of moving in to the mansion in December 1902, the Carnegies hosted their first party, an inaugural dinner for the "Carnegie veterans"—the Pittsburgh men who had worked together as partners in Carnegie's various enterprises prior to the sale of Carnegie Steel. When the time came for dinner, Carnegie led them to the dining room through an aisle formed by two lines of servants all dressed in Highland tartan, while Angus MacPherson, the Skibo bagpiper, serenaded the party. The oval table was covered in pink roses, orchids, and ferns from the conservatory, and throughout the meal the organist in the front hall played Scottish airs. The dinner, meant "to keep alive and cement the friendships" made during years of working together, became an annual occasion and a highlight of Carnegie's calendar.

During the nearly half a century that the Carnegies lived in the mansion, the building witnessed many such events. Scores of famous men and women—statesmen, authors, scientists, and other leaders—gathered around the table, often joined by a coterie of the friends Carnegie had lured to the neighborhood to become his Carnegie Hill neighbors. Carnegie's affable entertaining was enmeshed with his business transactions, his keen self-promotion, and his literary career. Each year on his birthday, he welcomed the press to the mansion for a kind of state-of-the-union according to Carnegie. The mansion served as Carnegie's stage in later life, and Louise, in her more modest way, carried on many of his traditions in the decades after his death.

Above all, the mansion functioned as a family home, a place to raise their beloved daughter. Here Margaret grew up, was first schooled, had her society debut, was courted, married, and even eventually gave birth to her first child.

To operate at such a scale, encompassing a multi-million-dollar charitable organization, extensive entertaining and concerts, and a privileged family home life, the building was designed to run like a machine. It served as a home and workplace for some two dozen servants. And technologically it enjoyed state-of-the-art heating, ventilating, and cooling systems; the latest in fireproof and steel construction; sophisticated internal and external communications systems; and the most up-to-date electrical lighting fixtures and appliances.

This remarkable behind-the-scenes operation, designed to support the activities of the family's three principal living and entertaining floors, spanned three additional floors in the mansion: the top or fourth floor of the house and two below-ground floors. In the end, each room had its function, its part to play in the theater of the Carnegies' mansion.

OPPOSITE One of the carved oak ceiling coffers of the main hall.

ABOVE Detail of the cornice in the mansion's entrance hall. For years the beautiful Caen stone of this hall was hidden under layers of paint, but it has now been restored.

MAIN FLOOR

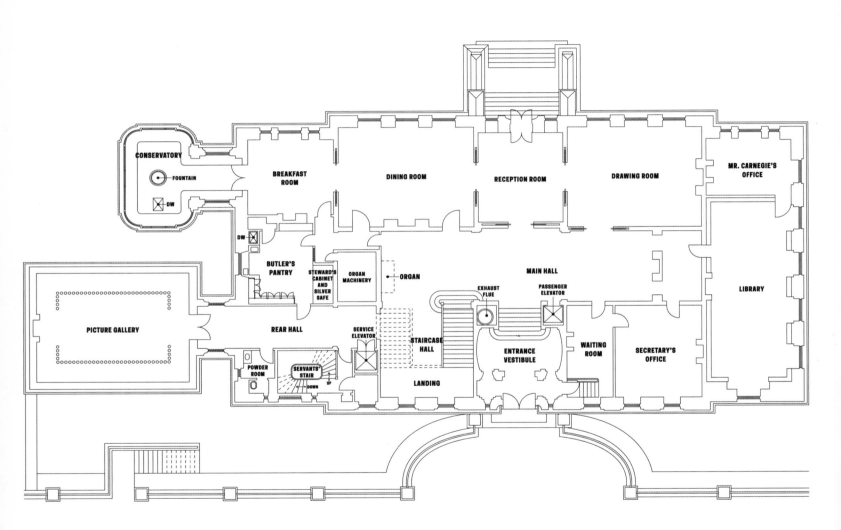

CONSERVATORY

FOUNTAIN

DW

BREAKFAST ROOM

DINING ROOM

RECEPTION ROOM

DRAWING ROOM

MR. CARNEGIE'S OFFICE

DW

BUTLER'S PANTRY

STEWARD'S CABINET AND SILVER SAFE

ORGAN MACHINERY

ORGAN

MAIN HALL

EXHAUST FLUE

PASSENGER ELEVATOR

LIBRARY

PICTURE GALLERY

REAR HALL

SERVICE ELEVATOR

STAIRCASE HALL

ENTRANCE VESTIBULE

WAITING ROOM

SECRETARY'S OFFICE

POWDER ROOM

SERVANTS' STAIR

UP

DOWN

LANDING

ENTRANCE

There were two ways to experience the Carnegie Mansion as a visitor. If you were coming to see the family, the liveried footman who answered the massive bronze doors would direct you straight ahead, through a second set of doors, up the stairs, and into the great front hall.

If, however, you were coming because you had an appointment with Carnegie's secretary to discuss the donation of an organ to your church, for example, or to present the case for why your town needed a library, your path into the house was a different one. Once inside the front door, you would be ushered to the right, up a small flight of stairs, and into a paneled waiting room (these spaces no longer exist in the mansion today).

The servant whose job it was to answer the door must have been incredibly busy. Up to 200 people a day showed up at the mansion. There were clergymen, college presidents, women representing various charitable causes, and many others. Some had appointments, but most were just hoping for money, or for a chance to shake the hand of the richest man in the world.

One such visitor recalled being greeted at the front door by a "servant wearing a waistcoat like Joseph's coat of many colors." He was guided through a "small, barred door at the side of the vestibule," which opened onto "a narrow passage and a flight of several steps. The steps lead into a small, low chamber, containing chairs, a table furnished with stationery and a few rich ornaments. The woodwork is dark and polished." It reminded him of

The entrance hall to the Carnegie Mansion in 2001. The door visible at right once led to the waiting room for visitors hoping to meet Carnegie or his secretaries.

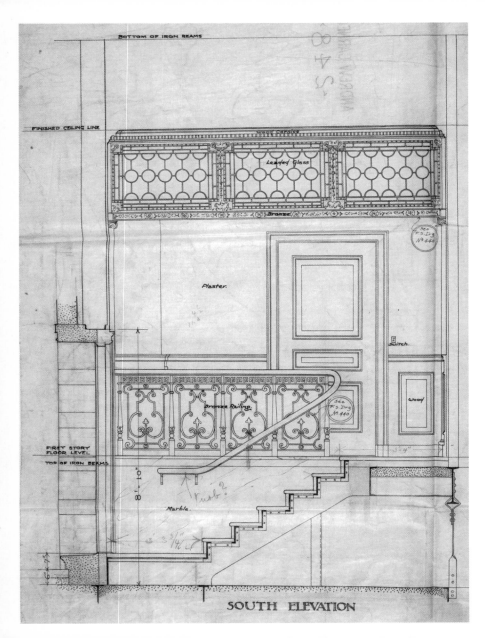

SOUTH ELEVATION

"those secret passages which were built into some medi-aeval castles for the quiet removal of unwelcome guests."

James Bertram, a fellow Scotsman, had become Andrew Carnegie's secretary in 1897 at the age of twenty-five, when Carnegie was looking for someone to help him manage his rapidly growing publishing career, philanthropic efforts, and voluminous correspondence. Bertram followed his employer to New York and established himself there, raising a family and serving as the first secretary and as a trustee of Carnegie Corporation of New York from the time of its inception in 1911 until his death in 1934. At the mansion he acted as the principal gatekeeper for Carnegie, assessing the multitudes who sought out the great man for charitable gifts. Bertram played a major role in systematizing Carnegie's philanthropy and in helping to determine the allocation of the money, both during Carnegie's lifetime and afterward through Carnegie Corporation. His office hummed with activity.

Babb, Cook & Willard's drawing of the waiting room.

In the lobby outside Carnegie's library-office, the paneled walls were lined with images of various benefactions that Carnegie had endowed.

Andrew Carnegie dictating to James Bertram the deed of gift for the branch library system of the New York Public Library, in his library at 5 West 51st Street, 1901.

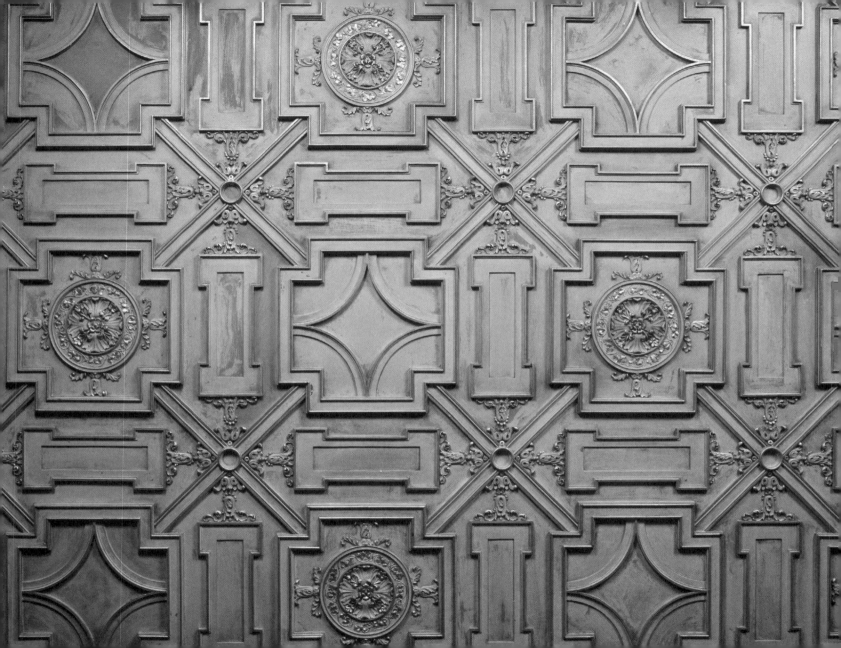

LIBRARY

Beyond Bertram's office lay the library of the house. From the beginning of the design process for the mansion, Carnegie had insisted that his library face Central Park. And so Howard Russell Butler devoted the building's entire west end to Carnegie's library, with "the southwest corner being walled off to make a *sanctum sanctorum*." The door openings here were a foot shorter than those for the other rooms in the mansion. Visitors to Carnegie's domain were meant to accommodate themselves to his (five-foot-two) vantage point.

The library and study walls were hung with gilt canvas above the paneled wainscot. At ceiling height, an elaborately stenciled frieze featuring Carnegie's favorite quotations, the inspirations he drew on in daily life, encircled

Artist Elmer Ellsworth Garnsey, who had a firm on Park Avenue and specialized in decorative work for public buildings, managed the furnishing of the mansion and also executed this library frieze.

OPPOSITE The ceiling in the library.

the room. He was a voracious reader, had memorized much of the output of Scotland's favorite poet, Robert Burns, and loved to recite other favorites as well, especially Shakespeare, Wordsworth, and the Bible. Carnegie's passion for literature was reflected overhead; "The chief glory of a nation," read one scroll, "is its authors." High above the fireplace was the phrase "Let there be light." Directly over the mantel was a carving in the shape of an open book (no longer extant), a duplicate of a design first created for Skibo Castle, inscribed with the motto "He that cannot reason is a fool; He that will not is a bigot; He that dares not is a slave." The walls of the library and study were covered with many pictures, certificates, and awards recognizing Carnegie's beneficence. Also hanging on the wall was the first investment Carnegie ever made: ten shares of stock in the Monongahela Insurance Company of Pittsburgh.

The library was the hub of Carnegie's working life. It was here that he conducted his philanthropic work, held meetings, and wrote his articles, speeches, and books when he was in New York. (He found he did his best writing in a little cottage retreat on the Skibo property, where he and his family spent a few weeks each summer getting away from their many houseguests.) And it was here that Carnegie Corporation of New York was established and run in its first years.

Carnegie never credited his success to endless hard work or talent. He knew as a driven young man that he had been in the right place at the right time, but once he was established, his days were weighted more toward pleasure. After breakfast (an ideal one for him was baked apples, oatmeal, and chicken), Carnegie spent a few hours each weekday morning that he was in residence in New York (generally October to May, with some time out over the Christmas/New Year period to see his sister-in-law on Cumberland Island in South Carolina) in the library with his secretary dealing with his correspondence and other business matters. He believed in exercise every day. He had a gym on the mansion's third floor, and he often enjoyed a late morning outing to the Saint Andrew's Golf Club in Westchester County. Lunch was fish or chicken, or oysters when in season, followed by two spoonfuls of "old scotch." In the afternoons when he was at home, after a nap he typically took a stroll in Central Park, frequently in the company of a friend or associate. He tried to keep his business appointments to the hour between 4:30 p.m. and 5:30 p.m. An ideal dinner was soup and oysters, but no meat, followed by a simple pudding like tapioca, and two more spoonfuls of scotch. Bedtime was 10:00 or 10:30 p.m.

But the library wasn't just an office. It represented his highest ideals, the true dreams of his childhood: to have a literary career, to be a man of letters. As one of his friends recalled, "He lived from boyhood onward in communion with books."

OPPOSITE The library, 1911.

All that man has thought or done... served as if by magic in book...

The dainties bred in a book lead th... mind from shade to sunshine...

...let there be light

A sketch of Andrew Carnegie by Orlando Rouland, 1911. Rouland studied Carnegie carefully in preparation for a portrait for the Carnegie Institution in Washington, D.C. He said that Carnegie was always "immaculately dressed" and was "very vain of his exceedingly small hands and feet and of his ears, which were set very close to his head."

Andrew Carnegie at the rolltop desk in his study. The desk was so large that it stayed in the house after the sale of all of the other Carnegie possessions in the late 1940s. For many years it was the desk of the librarian for the New York School of Social Work (now the Columbia University School of Social Work), which occupied the house in the 1950s and 1960s. It was only when the Smithsonian took over the mansion that the desk was removed (by taking out one of the windows and lowering the desk to the garden). Today it is housed with Cooper Hewitt's collections.

PHILANTHROPY

> *Surplus wealth is a sacred trust which its possessor is bound to administer in his lifetime for the good of the community.*
>
> —Andrew Carnegie, 1889

Andrew Carnegie revolutionized philanthropy. Over the course of his life he directed the donation of some $350 million, and from the Carnegie Mansion he established Carnegie Corporation of New York in 1911, to which he transferred the bulk of his remaining fortune, ensuring the continuation of that "sacred trust" after his death.

He was most proud of his work donating public library buildings. As a young teenager in Pittsburgh, Carnegie's world was transformed by the private library of Colonel James Anderson—who had opened his home and offered lending privileges to working boys. These books enriched Carnegie's self-education, and this early experience convinced him that there was no better use of one's money than to create public libraries for "boys and girls who have good within them and ability and ambition to develop it."

In keeping with his desire to aid the children of the workingman, Carnegie believed strongly in technical education. While he was friends with dozens of university presidents, most of whom appealed to him for endowment support, he trained his energies instead on small colleges and technical training institutes, like Booker T. Washington's Tuskegee Institute. In 1900 he established the Carnegie Technical Schools (later the Carnegie Institute of Technology and today Carnegie Mellon University) for the sons of steelworkers in Pittsburgh. It was modeled after New York's Cooper Union for the Advancement of Science and Art, which Carnegie had been actively supporting for years.

With most gifts, Carnegie insisted upon some kind of matching contribution. A city could receive monies for a library building, for example, if it committed to funding the building's maintenance and purchase the books. Berea College in Kentucky received $200,000—which in 1908 was Carnegie's largest sum to date given at one time to any institute of higher education—

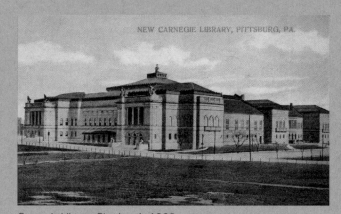

Carnegie Library, Pittsburgh, 1908.

provided it could raise the matching amount. In this way, Carnegie sought to leverage his investments and simultaneously encourage a kind of municipal self-improvement, such as he, the self-made man, had practiced himself.

He established Carnegie Corporation of New York in 1911 "to promote the advancement and diffusion of knowledge and understanding among the people of the United States." It was at the time the largest individual charitable trust ever created. According to lawyer and statesman Elihu Root, Carnegie at first intended to establish the foundation in his will, but when he realized that this would likely result in challenges, he decided to do it in his lifetime. Although his deed of gift was visionary in the authority it vested in the trustees to determine the foundation's policies and direction, Carnegie ran the charity in the early years as if it were still his own money, making decisions with an executive committee that consisted of his secretary, Bertram, and his financial adviser, Robert A. Franks; it was not until 1915, when Carnegie's health failed, that control went to the trustees. In 1919, after his death, the foundation gained its first salaried president. Today Carnegie Corporation of New York remains one of the most influential private foundations in the world. It has an endowment of around $3 billion, making grants focused on reforming education, strengthening democracy, and advancing international peace.

LEFT Carnegie provided the funds to build the Peace Palace, in The Hague, Netherlands, as well as endow it with a library of international law. The building opened in 1913.

Andrew Carnegie with Booker T. Washington and others at the twenty-fifth anniversary of the founding of the Tuskegee Institute in Alabama, 1906.

MAIN HALL

Carnegie took his inspiration for the entrance hall from the great halls of castles in Scotland, with their grand staircases. Yet he wanted something American, and something suitable for a gentleman, not a lord. When Howard Russell Butler recommended marble walls, Carnegie rejected the idea, thinking "it savored too much of palaces." Butler then proposed hanging the walls with Aubusson tapestries, but Carnegie refused that, as well, as the tapestries were not made in America. Carnegie decided instead to have an ornate coffered oak ceiling, and paneled oak woodwork on the walls, using oak that is said to have been carved and prepared in Scotland. The oak's dark tone, which Mrs. Carnegie personally selected, resulted in an overall darkness in the space, leading Howard Russell Butler to consider the hall one of the house's least successful spaces. Because the hall ran through the center of the building, the only source of natural light in the space came from the windows on the great stair. Some filtered light came as well from the stained-glass tympanum and roundels on the south wall over the entrance to the reception room.

The hall in Carnegie's time was decorated with furniture, and the teak parquet flooring was overlaid with heavy Oriental rugs. A bronze copy of a Renaissance statue of Mercury, god of commerce and trade, guarded the hall—a symbol no doubt of Carnegie's self-made fortune, and one that likely had special significance as a reference to Carnegie's early history as a messenger

RIGHT One of the Caldwell ceiling fixtures in the main hall.
OPPOSITE The main hall, looking west toward the library, 1938.

An elaborate custom-made frieze, of gilded canvas covered with a gessoed pattern and then painted with a metallic paint, runs above the paneled woodwork on the walls of the great hall. Most of the major rooms in the house had unusual custom-made wall coverings, many of which had a base of gilded canvas.

himself, working in the Pennsylvania Railroad's telegraph office. At one end of the hall was an enormous Aeolian organ. At the other end was an impressive marble fireplace, which may have been entirely decorative. On the fireplace wall hung two plaster casts from the Elgin marbles, a popular decoration at the turn of century.

Music was a central part of Andrew Carnegie's life, and this hall was often the source of such entertainments. At Christmas, choirs sang carols and hymns, including such Carnegie favorites as "Silent Night" and "Adeste Fidelis." Carnegie mostly kept his distance from organized religion, though he was a member of the Madison Avenue Presbyterian Church, where Henry Sloane Coffin was the minister. Louise Carnegie's family, the Whitfields, were members of the Church of the Divine Paternity, a Unitarian Universalist congregation (today the Fourth Universalist Society of New York); the pastor married Andrew and Louise. Louise and their daughter, Margaret, both regular churchgoers, became members of the Brick Presbyterian Church (today at Park Avenue and 91st Street, but prior to 1940 located at Fifth Avenue and 37th Street). Coffin and William Pierson Merrill of the Brick Church officiated at Margaret's 1919 wedding in the mansion.

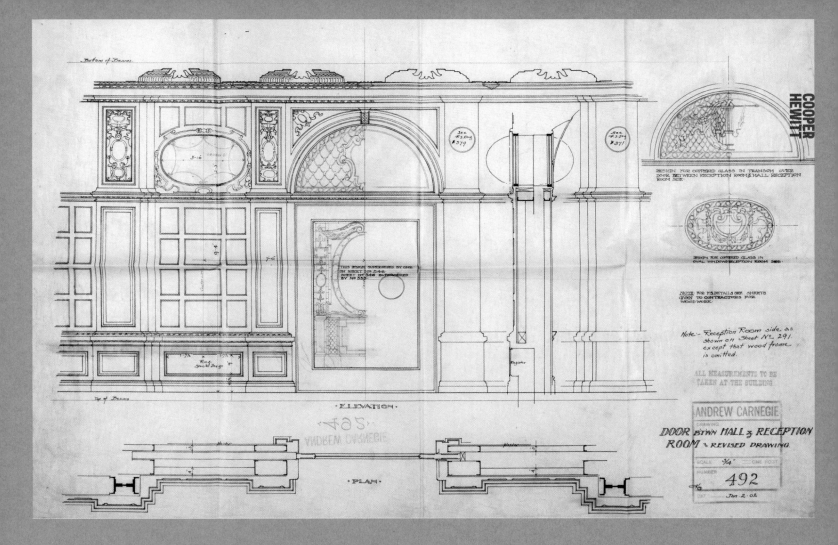

Babb, Cook & Willard's drawing of the south wall of the main hall.
The door to the reception room was originally designed with a large
decorative glass window, in order to increase the light into the hall.

THE ORGAN

Early every morning when the Carnegies were in residence in New York, Walter C. Gale, a well-known organist from the Broadway Tabernacle, would come to the mansion to play. Carnegie liked to be awakened to the music, and to have it accompany him as he dressed and prepared for the day. The sounds were designed to reached upstairs even to his bathroom. According to his secretary, James Bertram, Carnegie "would drink in the morning organ music. He would come downstairs walking on air. . . . Listening to the organ was a form of devotion for him."

The organ was commissioned from the Votey Organ Company in 1900 and was outfitted with newly patented Pneumatic Windchests and Electro-Pneumatic Action. It was first quoted at $15,800, though various alterations later increased that figure (one of the few issues Carnegie had with his new house was the organ's insufficiently grand bass register).

Carnegie believed that "music is a religion." His love of music shaped not only the interiors of his personal residences, but also his philanthropic efforts. While he did not feel he could be responsible for what was said from a pulpit, and thus was wary of giving to religious establishments, he did embrace the elevating power of music. Over the course of his life Carnegie donated thousands of organs to churches of various denominations across the English-speaking world.

An invitation to a series of 1937 organ recitals, written on Mrs. Carnegie's calling card. The family held organ recitals on a regular basis, a tradition that Mrs. Carnegie continued to the end of her life.

The organ, with the elegant carved door to the organ mechanicals room, and the service corridor to the left, showing false or decorative exposed pipes.

This chandelier was the showpiece of the mansion's grand paneled stair, depicted here in 2002, which connected the family's two principal living spaces. (The servants used a separate enclosed stair that connected all the floors of the house.)

CALDWELL LIGHTING

The lighting in the Carnegie Mansion represented the latest fashion. It was all electric, designed by Edward F. Caldwell & Company, one of the most prominent firms capitalizing on this new technology.

Edward F. Caldwell (1851–1914), originally a portrait painter, got his start in the 1880s as a lighting designer at Archer & Pancoast, one of the top U.S. gaslight fixtures companies. As Thomas Alva Edison's research paved the way for electrification on a large scale in the 1890s, companies like Archer & Pancoast began adapting to this technology, and Caldwell designed electric lighting for the New York State Building at the World's Columbian Exposition (1893) and the Boston Public Library (1895). The success of these projects enabled Caldwell to set up his own company in 1895. He focused on designing especially for electricity—adapting historical styles and traditional ornamentation to suit his exclusive clientele. The firm enjoyed tremendous success, designing fixtures for public buildings throughout the country, including the White House in 1902, St. Patrick's Cathedral in 1903, and Radio City Music Hall, Rockefeller Center, and the Waldorf-Astoria in the 1930s.

Today the Cooper Hewitt, Smithsonian Design Library holds the Caldwell Company archive (1895–1959), which encompasses more than 37,000 images and more than 13,000 presentation drawings.

This cast-bronze chandelier, depicted in a ca. 1902 photo from the Caldwell Company archive, features glass globe shades and decorative strapwork. It was one of many electric fixtures that Edward F. Caldwell & Company designed for the Carnegie Mansion.

The garden, with the rockery in the foreground, and the pergola at right, ca. 1903.

THE GARDEN

One of the most notable features of the Carnegie Mansion property was the extensive garden. For a couple who had enjoyed their courtship riding horses in Central Park, having views of and easy access to the outdoors was essential. It had been one of Louise's favorite parts of life at Cluny, the first Scottish castle they summered in. "From my little sitting room, steps lead right to the lawn, and Andrew's business room opens from my sitting room; so we slip from each other's rooms and out to the lawn with the greatest ease," she wrote to her mother from Scotland. "We mean to have a garden just like this when we get our place near N.Y. We shall have a Scotch gardener and have it as much like this as possible."

Howard Russell Butler, who planned the house so that the principal rooms all overlooked the garden, hired the noted Boston architect and landscape architect Guy Lowell to design it. Trained at the Massachusetts Institute of Technology, Harvard, and the École des Beaux-Arts, with a stint of landscape study at the Royal Botanic Gardens, Kew, Lowell was classically educated and well connected, with a father-in-law who was the first director of Harvard's Arnold Arboretum. By 1901, two years into his practice, while also teaching landscape design at the Massachusetts Institute of Technology, he had established a New York office. His influential book, *American Gardens* (1902), which focused on the traditions of Italian Renaissance garden design and their application for American gardens, followed a year later.

The work of designing the Carnegie garden fell to Richard Schermerhorn Jr., a Brooklyn native trained in civil engineering. Schermerhorn followed Lowell's precepts by designing a formal garden close to the house, which provided a transition from architecture to garden, and by creating a more romantic, rambling area in the main garden.

The large open central lawn was surrounded by winding paths and flower beds. At the eastern end of the garden was a landscaped rockery, or rock garden, which is still extant. Some of the original plantings included wisteria (still a favorite aspect of the building's south facade today), azaleas, rhododendron, roses, and

The rockery, 2001.

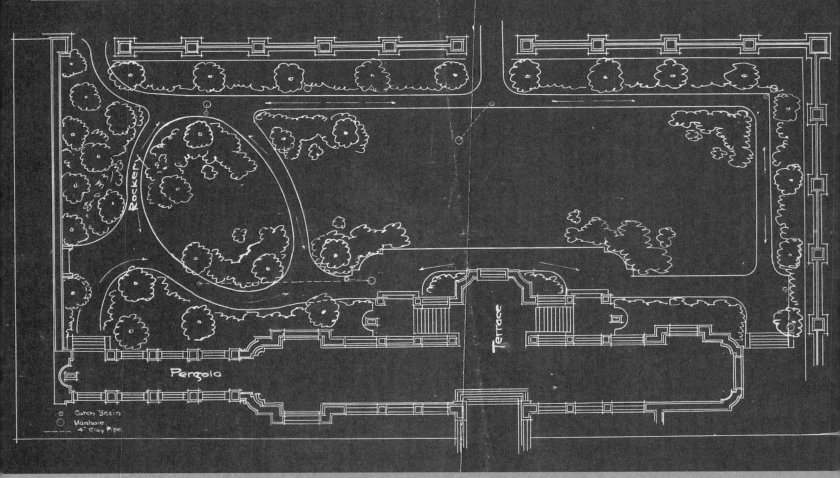

Garden for Andrew Carnegie.
90th St - 5th Ave - N.Y.C.

Rockery

Terrace

Pergola

Catch Basin
Manhole
4" Clay Pipe

Richard Schermerhorn's design for the Carnegie garden, 1901.

ivy. Carnegie's favorites were red geraniums. Trees included chestnuts, large poplars, sugar maples, elms, and various flowering trees. The trees were most thickly planted along the garden's eastern perimeter, to create a screen of privacy from the other houses on 90th and 91st Streets.

The garden, envisioned as a playland for the Carnegies' precious child, was a source of endless enjoyment and became an integral part of the family's life in the mansion.

Margaret as a young girl.

The wisteria on the house, one of the original plantings, shown here in 2002.

RECEPTION ROOM

The first of the public rooms entered was the reception room. This room, whose square shape Mrs. Carnegie had chosen, was placed between the two principal rooms, the dining room and the drawing room, and provided access to the garden. Arranged as a parlor, with myriad sofas, a Turkish carpet, and many plants, it was an ideal place for the ladies of the house to receive company. The room originally had a cream and pale yellow color scheme and was illuminated by five crystal chandeliers.

ABOVE The room features a stained-glass tympanum window attributed to Louis Comfort Tiffany.

The reception room, open to the garden, 1938.

The drawing room was the setting for this photo documenting the founding meeting of Carnegie Corporation of New York in 1911. Mrs. Carnegie and Margaret were included; they both later served as trustees, Mrs. Carnegie from 1920 to 1930, and Margaret from 1935 to 1973 and then as honorary trustee until her death in 1990. In the center of the back row is Carnegie's secretary, James Bertram, who served the foundation from its founding until his death in 1934.

OPPOSITE LEFT The drawing room in 1938.
OPPOSITE RIGHT The elaborate plaster ceiling decorations included bagpipes, a reference to Carnegie's native Scotland and Mrs. Carnegie's favorite music.

To the right of the square reception room lay the drawing room. When Howard Russell Butler first discussed the plans with the Carnegies, he suggested that after determining the dimensions of the dining room, the second step in designing the house was the ballroom. "This," according to Butler, "made Carnegie furious. 'I will never have a ball-room in any house of mine,' he exclaimed." And so the ballroom was rechristened the drawing room. Laid out with the same dimensions as the dining room, the room was decorated in the manner of Louis XV, with carved boiserie paneling that was painted ivory and gilded, and corner niches with gilded shell motifs. The coved plaster ceiling featured decorations of musical instruments, which sometimes led to the room's being referred to as the music room, and the walls were covered with rose-colored silk damask. The room was furnished with French antiques and was lit by a crystal chandelier and wall sconces.

The ornate decorative scheme, which shared stylistic qualities with Mrs. Carnegie's suite of rooms upstairs, reflected this space's function as a place primarily for women. After formal dinners, female guests would retire here for conversation, while the men remained in the dining room.

DINING ROOM

To the left of the reception room lay the dining room. This room, which was the first to be planned in the house, set the measurements for much of the rest of the ground floor. Even before an architect had been selected, Howard Russell Butler told a bewildered Carnegie that he needed to determine the size of the room. "If you leave the size of your dining-room to an architect," Butler explained, "the first time you give a dinner party you will either say, 'Why did this architect give us a room so small that it will not hold our guests?' or you will say, 'Why did he build such a barn of a dining-room?'" It was Louise who quickly understood what was at stake. There would be twenty-two at dinner, she decided, and thus the room was fixed at thirty-six by twenty-five feet.

Carnegie loved to entertain, and he was never more at home in New York than when he was holding forth in this room. For him the best company was that of writers, statesmen, and scientists, not his fellow industrialists or bankers. As one friend recalled, "He delighted in the society of the learned and the witty. He gathered about him those whom he held in respect for their knowledge of literature, science, and affairs." His acquaintances were legion. He often ate before one of his large dinner parties, "to avoid indigestible food, and talk while others were eating."

For formal evenings Carnegie enjoyed creating an atmosphere of great ceremony. On certain occasions, he imported the Skibo tradition of having the party follow the bagpiper around the main rooms of the house before marching into the dining room. He organized a series of annual evenings, such as the Carnegie veterans gathering or the "Knights of the Cloth" literary dinner—so called because each guest would be asked to sign on the table-cloth. Each Knights of the Cloth dinner was held in one man's honor. It was customary for guests to toast the guest of honor, a tradition that Carnegie's competitiveness often escalated into something of a contest of wits. The toast was evidently a task that some guests dreaded; when the esteemed naturalist John Burroughs wrote to accept the invitation to a 1904 dinner in honor of the great English Liberal statesman John Morley, he said, about "that after dinner speaking . . . excuse me, will you not Mr. Carnegie? I know you will. Sincerely yours, John Burroughs."

The room featured dark Circassian walnut linenfold paneling, over which was an iridescent damask wall covering. Above the green serpentine marble fireplace Howard Russell Butler installed one of his own paintings. Two doors on the north wall served different purposes; the one to the west, which led to the front hall, was for the guests. The other, connected to the pantry, where a dumbwaiter brought warm food from the kitchen below, was for the servants.

OPPOSITE The dining room, 1938.

TABLECLOTH

The Carnegies had a tradition at special dinners that called for each guest to sign his or her name on the tablecloth in pencil. Servants later embroidered these signatures onto the linen damask, creating a permanent record of the event and the impressive roster of guests. Two of these cloths are in the collections of Cooper Hewitt, and another now resides in the collections of the Museum of the City of New York. Some were used over the course of decades, for multiple dinners, and contain dozens of names. Among them are Mark Twain, Marie Curie, and several U.S. presidents.

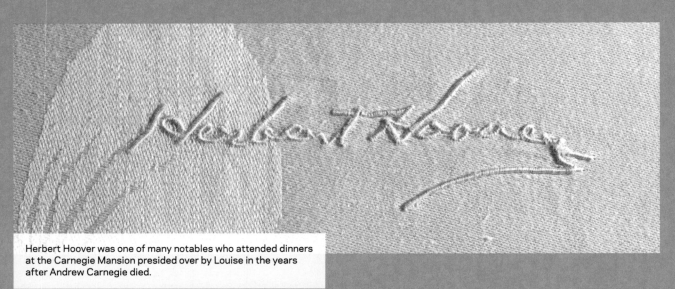

Herbert Hoover was one of many notables who attended dinners at the Carnegie Mansion presided over by Louise in the years after Andrew Carnegie died.

BREAKFAST ROOM

The other room overlooking the garden was the breakfast room. Having a dining room that seated twenty-two meant that a smaller room was needed for family meals—and so it was decided to create a breakfast room to the east, adjacent to the conservatory, "placed so as to get the early morning sunlight." The room was adorned with bronze fixtures with Tiffany glass, the windows had louvered shutters, and the buffet sideboard matched the Circassian walnut wall paneling. Here too was a custom-designed wall covering, as well as a molded plaster ceiling with a raised gilded pattern of decorative geometric strapwork.

In this modest room Margaret Carnegie was married on April 22, 1919—the thirty-second anniversary of Andrew and Louise's wedding—in a small ceremony attended only by family and close friends. Louise secretly arranged for Angus MacPherson to come over from Skibo for the occasion, so that Margaret could awaken on her wedding day to the sound of the bagpipes. Carnegie was by then very frail and weak, but he managed, in one of his last semipublic appearances, to escort his daughter down the main staircase and through the suite of public rooms, accompanied by the sounds of the organ.

The breakfast room, 1938.

CONSERVATORY

From the breakfast room, Palladian bronze and glass doors opened onto a freestanding iron and glass structure known as the conservatory. Situated to capture the morning light, the conservatory provided the family with plants and flowers throughout the winter. Howard Russell Butler designed a rockery for the southern end, with a rustic, grotto-like backdrop made of cork. A marble fountain stood in the center of the room. The conservatory had its own separate heating and ventilating system as well as a small elevator to the potting shed located below.

The conservatory, with its rockery, 1938.

A whimsical hummingbird spigot.

PICTURE GALLERY

At the eastern end of the house lay a separate one-story extension containing the picture gallery, a large, high-ceilinged room lit from above by an elegant white-glass skylight. "Our picture gallery here will surprise you when you see it," Andrew Carnegie wrote to the director of the new Carnegie Institute in Pittsburgh (now the Carnegie Museum of Art), soon after moving into the house in December 1902.

Carnegie did not collect important Old Master pictures, as many of his associates did, Morgan and Frick in particular. The family chose paintings that they liked, mostly from living artists, and they did not spend a lot of money on their acquisitions. Carnegie was also often friendly with the artists. Fellow Scotsman Alexander Roche, for example, who painted a portrait of Louise and Margaret soon after the family settled in the mansion, inscribed his name on the tablecloth at one of the famed Carnegie dinners. Edwin Austin Abbey, whose *Stony Ground* of 1884 (now in the Brooklyn Museum) was the first painting Carnegie purchased, accompanied Carnegie on one of his coaching trips in Scotland.

The picture gallery, sometimes called the music room, also contained a piano that Margaret played and was the site of numerous important family events. In 1913, in preparation for Margaret's debutante party, Mrs. Carnegie's brother, the architect Henry Whitfield, was brought in to undertake renovations to connect the gallery to the suite of public rooms along the south front, via the conservatory, for optimum entertaining. Originally the picture gallery was accessed only via the corridor that led from the great hall. As the province of the servants—the back of house, in a way—containing the butler's pantry, a bathroom, the elevator, and the servants' stair, this corridor was a less-than-ideal route for guests. Whitfield extended the picture gallery seven feet in the direction of the garden and connected it with the conservatory, creating a new means of circulation. In the process, he moved the original marble fireplace from the east end of the room to this new south wall and created two large French windows on the east wall. Anticipating Margaret's coming-out party, the newspapers reported the "extensive alterations" appeared to be "a preliminary warning that a bud is about to blossom" and that the "beautiful magnificence" of the "transformed residence . . . is an appropriate background to the richest of debutantes."

Margaret's coming-out was a grand affair, with some 800 guests from all over the United States as well as England and France. "Well, the party is over and such a bright and happy party it has been, without a hitch or flaw," Louise wrote in her diary. "Baba had at least a hundred bouquets and baskets of flowers; a wonderful tribute to our little girl. . . . Party was over at 2 a.m., a very great success. Daddy very happy greeting guests." The picture gallery was the site of other such family events in subsequent years, such as the 1927 wedding of Miss Louise Whitfield (Mrs. Carnegie's niece, the daughter of the

architect Henry Whitfield) and the 1931 debutante party of another relative, Primrose Whitfield.

Christmas was a favorite family holiday, especially for Louise, who was described by her biographer as a woman "with Christmas eternally in her heart." The tree was always placed here in the picture gallery, and the room—along with much of the house—garlanded with holly and mistletoe. Several days before Christmas the servants' party was held around the tree, where "appropriate goodies were passed, gifts distributed, and good wishes exchanged." Mrs. Carnegie was extremely organized and kept extensive lists of people to whom she sent gifts. She wrapped the presents herself, piling them high on the billiard table upstairs in advance of the holiday. She also hosted an annual party for hundreds of students from International House, a residential community that opened in 1924 at 500 Riverside Drive with funding from John D. Rockefeller Jr. and other New York notables. There was lots of singing of carols around the tree. At her last such party, in 1945, after shaking hands with each and all, she spoke to the assembled: "Christmas means more to us this year than ever before for a new light is breaking over the world. . . . We need the joy of Christmas to lighten the deep sense of responsibility which rests upon us. Our nation has been given a second chance, and we must each do our part to see that we do not fail the world again."

OPPOSITE View of the toplit picture gallery, 1938. The coved ceiling was covered in metallic leaf, to enhance the reflected light.

SECOND FLOOR

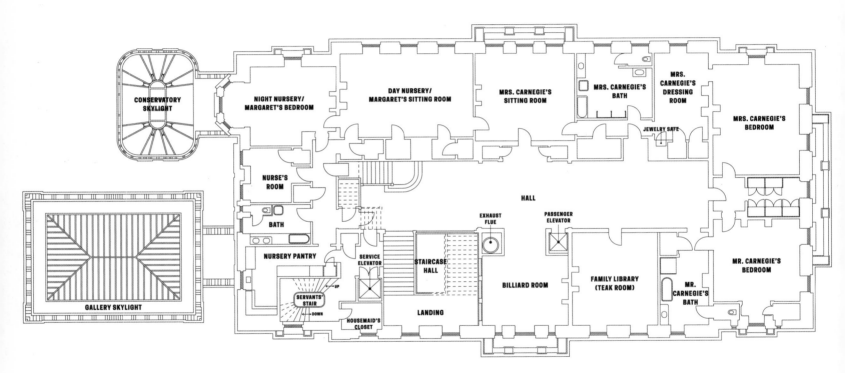

CONSERVATORY SKYLIGHT

NIGHT NURSERY/ MARGARET'S BEDROOM

DAY NURSERY/ MARGARET'S SITTING ROOM

MRS. CARNEGIE'S SITTING ROOM

MRS. CARNEGIE'S BATH

MRS. CARNEGIE'S DRESSING ROOM

MRS. CARNEGIE'S BEDROOM

JEWELRY SAFE

NURSE'S ROOM

BATH

HALL

GALLERY SKYLIGHT

NURSERY PANTRY

SERVICE ELEVATOR

STAIRCASE HALL

EXHAUST FLUE

PASSENGER ELEVATOR

FAMILY LIBRARY (TEAK ROOM)

BILLIARD ROOM

MR. CARNEGIE'S BEDROOM

MR. CARNEGIE'S BATH

SERVANTS' STAIR

UP

DOWN

HOUSEMAID'S CLOSET

LANDING

The second floor was mostly the domain of the family, as it contained the family bedrooms. There were, however, some entertaining rooms, such as the family library and the billiard room—which contained a rare English-style billiard table that Carnegie had made to order for the exorbitant price of $1,500. At the top of the grand stair, which apparently was adorned with a stuffed barracuda that Mr. Carnegie had caught off Key West, a central hall ran the length of the house. It was elegantly divided into several sections by means of carved oak beams and paired pilasters and columns. Bands of oak leaves and acorns appear as details throughout the house. This motif no doubt served as a reference both to Carnegie's Scottish heritage and to his self-made fortune. (The Vanderbilts, another family without an illustrious lineage or crest, had adopted the oak leaf and acorn as their heraldic symbol, in honor of the proverb "Mighty oaks from little acorns grow.") Here too was a decorative plaster ceiling with a raised strapwork design. The door openings on the hall were framed with highly decorative moldings and scrolls. In one corner of the hall was a small stair, with the same elegant balustrade as the main staircase, for the family to use to access the third floor, where Margaret's schoolroom, Andrew's gymnasium, and Louise's sister Stella Whitfield's living suite were located.

A balustrade detail on the second-floor railing of the grand staircase.

BEDROOMS

The women of the household occupied the second-floor rooms running along the garden, or south, front of the mansion. Mrs. Carnegie's bedroom was in the southwest corner of the building, overlooking both Central Park and the mansion garden. Adjacent to her room was a dressing room, with a jewel safe built into the wall, and a bathroom. Her sitting room and her daughter's sitting room abutted each other in the middle of the south facade and were both accessible directly from the hall, if either cared to entertain visitors in a more intimate, private setting.

Margaret's suite, located at the southeast corner of the house, contained a night nursery (later called her bedroom) and a day nursery (later referred to as her sitting room). There was also a small kitchen and a bed and bath for the child's nurse, "Nannie" Lockerbie. Lockerbie was the only servant who lived on the family's floor.

On evenings when there were parties, Mrs. Carnegie would dress and then visit her daughter. "Mother knew that I loved to see her before she went down to the drawing room to receive her guests," Margaret recalled in later years. Margaret did not see much of her father during her childhood. "But when I did, it was always exciting," she remembered. "He believed in Fairies, and made me believe in them too. When he gave me his soft long-drawn out whistle something for me was dropped in his pocket! At times other lovely mysterious presents were found under my pillow when I went to bed at night: amethyst, rose quartz, malachite, azurite, polished into the shape of an egg."

For more than two years Margaret was made something of an invalid by an unidentified bone disease. Her right leg was placed in a plaster cast and an iron brace, which had to be refitted periodically as she grew, and she was often carried around in a cart. Finally in the spring of 1908 she was able to get rid of the splint and plaster. Carnegie cried tears of joy when he saw his daughter walking. "He went to church with Mother and me the next Sunday which showed he was truly thankful I could walk again, because he seldom went to church," Margaret remembered. "What lovely clothes my Mother bought me to wear that spring!"

Mr. Carnegie's bedroom, which was located in the northwest corner of the house, overlooking Central Park, unfortunately appears not ever to have been photographed. Throughout his life he slept in the brass bed he had had as a child. This room included intricately carved decorative detailing in teak made to Lockwood de Forest's designs in India, linking the room stylistically to the adjacent family library.

OPPOSITE Mrs. Carnegie's bedroom, 1938. In an echo of the decor of the drawing room downstairs, Mrs. Carnegie's bedroom had a distinctly feminine and French-style decorative scheme, with carved flower festoons over the fireplace and the doors and an ornamental plasterwork ceiling. Interestingly, the herringbone pattern on the floor was laid down only around the perimeter; in the center of the room, where the large carpet lay, was plain hardwood plank flooring—a cost-saving trick employed in the south-facing rooms on this floor.

OPPOSITE Mrs. Carnegie's bathroom had a marble floor, a porcelain tub and sitz bath, and wicker furniture. All exposed bathroom pipes on the principal floors of the mansion were plated in silver.

ABOVE Margaret's bedroom, 1938.

ABOVE The Carnegies and their daughter, Margaret, in the mansion, on Margaret's eighteenth birthday.

LEFT Detail of the teak decorative carving in Mr. Carnegie's bedroom.

ANDREW CARNEGIE AND LOUIS COMFORT TIFFANY

Andrew Carnegie appears to have had a special appreciation of the artistic glass production of Louis Comfort Tiffany (1848-1933). Not only do photos of the Carnegie Mansion show Tiffany lamps in various locations—there are at least four table lamps and a turtleback chandelier in photos of the teak room alone—but Carnegie also had them sent over to Skibo Castle; there, in his house in Scotland, these lamps would have promoted American ingenuity and style while giving light.

More extraordinary was Carnegie's attempt to show off Tiffany's talents in Scotland by commissioning a landscape stained-glass window for the medieval abbey in Dunfermline, as a memorial to his parents and sibling. The fact that the firm communicated directly with Andrew Carnegie about this window, and not with Mrs. Carnegie or a subordinate, indicates Carnegie's personal interest.

Rejected as "unecclesiastical and too modern," the Tiffany window lay for nearly a quarter century packed up in a basement. It was only later installed in the Dunfermline Carnegie Hall auditorium. Today, restored, it is displayed at the headquarters of the Carnegie Dunfermline Trust. The window remains a testament to the extent of Carnegie's admiration for Tiffany glass.

COOPER HEWITT

This Tiffany dragonfly lamp, which can be seen in a photo of the library at Skibo Castle, was given to Cooper-Hewitt by Margaret Carnegie Miller. Interestingly, and not surprisingly for Carnegie, it was not retrofitted but started its life with electricity.

FAMILY LIBRARY (THE TEAK ROOM)

The most exceptional room in the Carnegie Mansion was the family library, or teak room, as it is affectionately known today. Distinguished from the rest of the house by its Indian-style teakwood interior decoration, it was designed by the painter and interior designer Lockwood de Forest (1845–1932). It featured carved teakwood paneling from India on the walls, fireplace surround, ceiling frieze, and corbels, and a matching carved teak cabinet, along with de Forest's Indian-inspired stenciled ornament on the walls and ceiling. The room is a remarkable example of the Indian taste that Lockwood de Forest made fashionable in the United States, beginning in 1881 and lasting until World War I. Commissions in this style included those in collaboration with Louis Comfort Tiffany, such as the Mark Twain House in Hartford, Connecticut, and others later obtained on his own, such as for Mary Elizabeth Garrett in Baltimore, Maryland, and Bryn Mawr College in Pennsylvania.

Howard Russell Butler initially hired Lockwood de Forest and the A. H. Davenport Company to do the interior decoration for the entire mansion. Butler and de Forest seem to have been quite good friends. They traveled with the same teacher and mentor, Frederic Church: de Forest to Italy and Greece in 1868–69 and Butler to Mexico in 1884. More important for the history of the teak room is the fact that they were colleagues in the American Society of Fine Arts, where Butler was

Lockwood de Forest, 1900–1910.

president and Lockwood de Forest and Louis Comfort Tiffany were among the stockholders; Andrew Carnegie, of course, approached by Butler in 1892, was one of the principal funders. The teak room and the Tiffany lamps that lit it can be seen as a product of Carnegie's patronage of artists of the Society of Fine Arts.

OPPOSITE The family library, 1938.

RIGHT AND OPPOSITE LEFT De Forest created stencils for wall and ceiling decorations using the patterns found in the pierced brass of stone *jalis* (screens) that were employed in Indian temples and houses. These created beautiful patterns of light while simultaneously protecting inhabitants from the strong sun. In the teak room de Forest cleverly chose a yellow varnish and a red tone for his stencils, to evoke the golden tones of the sun, the brass, and the red sandstone.
OPPOSITE RIGHT Carved corbels in the teak room. The differing tones of teak in the room indicate that de Forest likely used teak from both India and Burma.

Lockwood de Forest studied with Church while the celebrated painter was planning his Persian-inspired country home, Olana, in Hudson, New York. De Forest pored through Church's drawings for the house, as well as his source books on Persian and Oriental architecture.

The lives of de Forest and Tiffany intersected when they both joined Candace Wheeler and Samuel Colman in the formation of the Society of Decorative Arts (1877), which educated women in the field of design for decorative objects. In 1880, these designers worked together under the firm of Associated Artists. In the same year, de Forest joined Tiffany in a separate partnership. His first assignment was to return to Egypt and then go on to India in search of exotic interior furnishings. In the course of this year-and-a-half-long Indian trip, which was also his honeymoon, de Forest decided to forge his career as a decorative designer specializing in Indian furnishings. He set up a workshop in Ahmedabad in collaboration with a family of Jain merchants, the Hutheesings, who had a large number of *mistri* (master) craftsmen working for them. The Hutheesings also were related to or otherwise knew merchants who owned studios in other media, enabling de Forest to produce objects in teak and brass; stencil designs; and jewelry for export. He stayed long enough to become good friends with the Hutheesings

and entrust the business to them. De Forest devised a system of numbered designs on the backs of wood carvings, decorative brass elements, and stencils. One set was retained in the studio in Ahmedabad, and other sets were sent back to the United States, both to Tiffany and others who might order from him, and for de Forest's own studio and display rooms. De Forest took the inspiration for his designs from the long tradition of Gujarati carving in wood and stone, some early examples of which he found in eleventh-century Jain temples. His genius was to see what designs would appeal to the Western eye and to edit and craft their use to create a compelling exotic effect.

The teak room is the most intact de Forest interior commission still remaining in the place for which it was intended. It was one of only a select few in the country, an exotic and captivating treasure of a room, which would have made an enormous impression on visitors. Newly conserved in 2013, the room exudes a warm and appealing glow that must have provided, in Carnegie's day, the perfect environment for an intimate family gathering. As Margaret recalled in her diary, the family passed many evening hours together in this room, cranking the handle of their "Victor Talking Machine," listening to recordings of Scottish ballads and American folksongs. Margaret's favorite was Harry Lauder singing "I Love a Lassie."

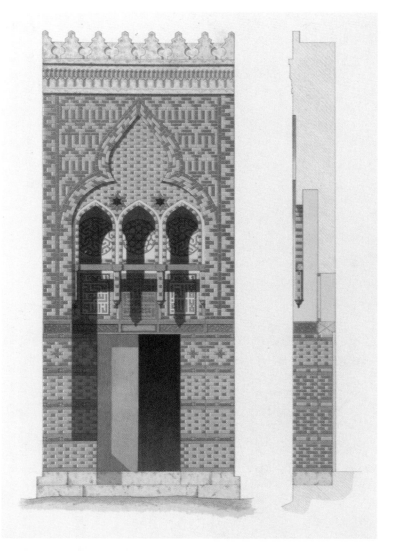

ABOVE Birbal's Palace at Fatehpur Sikri, which was opened for de Forest to paint in 1881. He wrote in his diary that it was "a perfect example of architecture of the time of Akbai [Akbar the Great, Mughal emperor from 1556 to 1605] and has been preserved just as it was." LEFT Pattern books like Jules Bourgoin's *Les Arts Arabes* (1873) undoubtedly stimulated de Forest's interest in the art and architecture of Persia and the Near East. This plate features the design for the entry to a mosque at Alexandria.

THIRD FLOOR

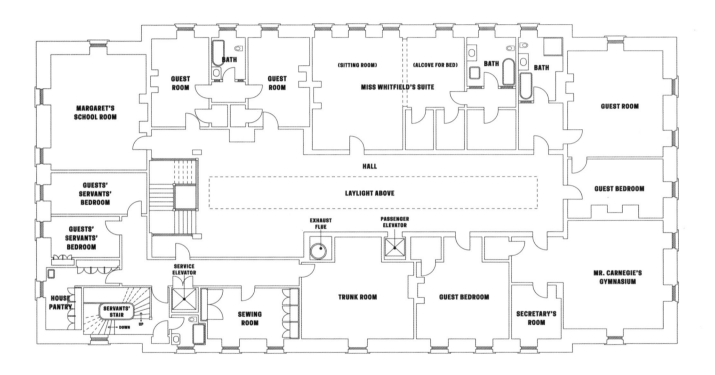

BATH

GUEST
ROOM

GUEST
ROOM

(SITTING ROOM)

(ALCOVE FOR BED)

BATH

BATH

GUEST ROOM

MARGARET'S
SCHOOL ROOM

MISS WHITFIELD'S SUITE

GUESTS'
SERVANTS'
BEDROOM

HALL

GUEST BEDROOM

LAYLIGHT ABOVE

GUESTS'
SERVANTS'
BEDROOM

EXHAUST
FLUE

PASSENGER
ELEVATOR

SERVICE
ELEVATOR

MR. CARNEGIE'S
GYMNASIUM

HOUSE
PANTRY

SERVANTS'
STAIR

DOWN

UP

SEWING
ROOM

TRUNK ROOM

GUEST BEDROOM

SECRETARY'S
ROOM

The third-floor hall was illuminated by a long stained-glass laylight, framed by an elaborate plaster molding. There were a number of guest bedrooms on this floor, as well as the living quarters of Louise Carnegie's sister, Stella Whitfield. Her rooms occupied the middle of the hall, overlooking the garden. She had a large living room with an elegant carved cornice; the room had a fireplace and extended into a bedroom alcove, with a bathroom and several closets, too. Stella came to live with the Carnegies in 1890, after the sisters' mother died. Louise and Stella's brother, Henry, also became part of the Carnegies' family at this time, although he was sent to boarding school; after attending college at Harvard, he married in 1902 and set up his own household, so he never lived at 2 East 91st Street. Stella was part of the household for two decades, before setting up on her own early in the war years; she continued to enjoy Skibo summers with the Carnegies until her death at the Scottish castle in 1928.

The third-floor hall, in the 1940s, with its coved ceiling and white-glass laylight.

Andrew, Louise, Stella, and Margaret walking in New York City, 1911.

The third floor had a schoolroom for Margaret, in the same corner of the house as her bedroom on the floor below, where she was tutored until she entered the Spence School at age thirteen. There the walls were covered with burlap mounted on carpet felt, so that drawings and lessons could be easily pinned up. There was also a trunk room and a sewing room, as well as a gymnasium for Andrew.

Carnegie's gymnasium, photographed here in the late 1940s, was located in the northwest corner of the house, directly above his bedroom, and had walls covered in quartered American oak. When he was unable to make the trip out to his beloved Saint Andrew's golf course in Westchester, he often practiced his putting here.

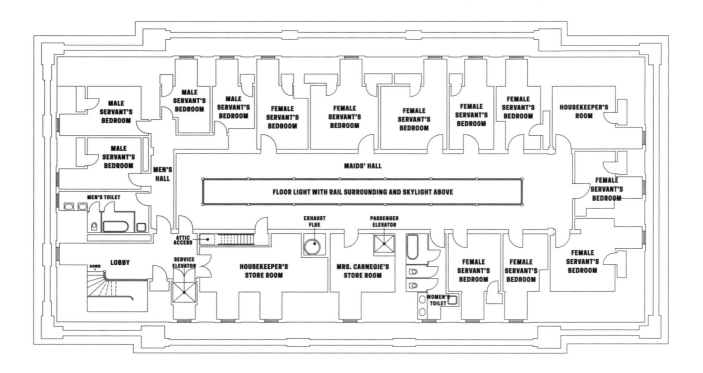

The smooth operation of the Carnegie household, contained on the three main floors, was made possible by the family's sizable staff. Their realm, behind the scenes, encompassed the top, or fourth, floor of the house, and the two lowest levels—the ground floor and the basement.

The skylit top floor of the mansion was given over to servants' quarters. The men were located at the southwest corner, and the women occupied much of the rest of the floor. Mrs. Nicoll, the housekeeper, had a large storeroom, adjacent to the elevator and the stair hall, and Mrs. Carnegie, too, had a small storeroom on this floor. The center of the hall floor was enclosed with a bronze balustrade, so the passage to the various rooms was quite narrow, only one person wide. The bulk of the hall was given over to a laylight of white leaded glass, which allowed light down to the third floor. A number of features immediately set this floor apart from the other living floors. The servants' floor did not enjoy the sophisticated ventilation system of the floors below, where each room could be individually adjusted; it had only steam radiators. There was no insulation, either, so these rooms were probably quite cold in the winters. Most servants would have spent the summers in Scotland, so they would at least have been spared the worst of the New York heat. The walls here did not have decorative treatments; they were tiled with white glazed brick, as in the ground floor and basement areas, to facilitate cleaning.

ABOVE LEFT The fourth-floor hall as it appeared in the 1940s.
BELOW LEFT Babb, Cook & Willard's design for the skylight at the top of the house.

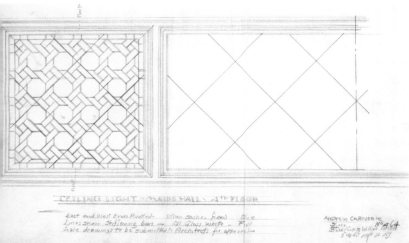

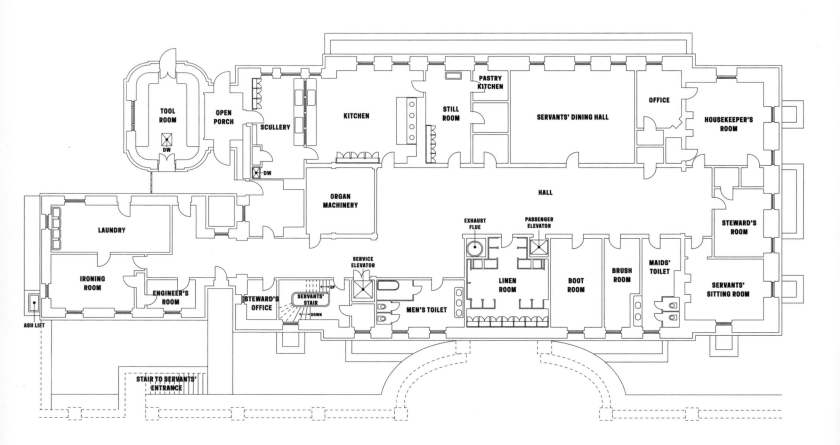

TOOL
ROOM

DW

OPEN
PORCH

SCULLERY

KITCHEN

STILL
ROOM

PASTRY
KITCHEN

SERVANTS' DINING HALL

OFFICE

HOUSEKEEPER'S
ROOM

DW

ORGAN
MACHINERY

HALL

STEWARD'S
ROOM

LAUNDRY

EXHAUST
FLUE

PASSENGER
ELEVATOR

IRONING
ROOM

ENGINEER'S
ROOM

SERVICE
ELEVATOR

STEWARD'S
OFFICE

SERVANTS'
STAIR

UP

DOWN

MEN'S TOILET

LINEN
ROOM

BOOT
ROOM

BRUSH
ROOM

MAIDS'
TOILET

SERVANTS'
SITTING ROOM

ASH LIFT

STAIR TO SERVANTS'
ENTRANCE

The ground floor, accessed by the servants' stair, contained the principal spaces needed to service the mansion and support the staff. Most all the rooms were lined with glazed white subway tiles for ease of cleaning. The eastern end of the floor, under the picture gallery, housed the laundry. Carnegie had specified that he didn't want any "steam-odors," so the starch boiler and the clothes boiler and the irons in the adjacent ironing room all ran on electricity. Underneath the conservatory was a tool room or potting shed. There was also a linen room, whose contents, according to a 1910 magazine article, spoke "of liberal-hearted entertaining"; a packing room, a boot room, and a brush room, used by Mr. Carnegie's valet for pressing the master's clothes, which featured an electric heater; and a room containing the organ machinery. The house also had its own intercommunicating telephone system, which functioned like an intercom, in addition to Carnegie's private telephone lines. Adjacent to the stair was the paneled room of the steward, who for many years was Alexander Morrison. This room also overlooked the servants' entrance from the outside of the mansion, enabling the steward to oversee the comings and goings of all the staff, and all deliveries.

The large kitchen was located underneath the dining room; one side was a scullery lined with vast marble sinks, and the other a still room and pastry cook's kitchen, as well as room for iceboxes, a larder, and cold storage. At the western end of the floor were the servants' living rooms. Their dining room or hall ran along the garden front. Mrs. Nicoll, the housekeeper, had her room on this floor. There were bathrooms for men and women. And there was a large servants' sitting room, with a floor and wainscoting of American oak.

THE SERVANTS

The Carnegies usually had around twenty-five servants at any given time—most of whom were Scottish and had first been hired to work at Skibo Castle. Many of them worked for the family for decades, traveling back and forth with the family between New York and Skibo. Of the four servants Carnegie singled out in his will "as members of the family," for example, Mrs. Nicoll, the head housekeeper, and housemaid Margaret "Maggie" Anderson were both hired in 1887, during Louise and Andrew's extended honeymoon; George Irvine, the butler, was hired the following summer; and Agnes "Nannie" Lockerbie was hired in 1898, after the birth of the Carnegies' child.

Maggie Anderson retired in 1912, after twenty-three years with the family. The retirement party held in her honor was reported on in papers across the country—a story Carnegie no doubt placed in order to promote his image as a paternalistic, benevolent employer. Carnegie presented Anderson with a gold watch, a life pension of $500 a year, and a round-trip ticket to San Francisco, so she could visit her brother, her only living relative, before going back home to Edinburgh, where she intended to buy a public house

Martha "Mattie" Clarke, born in Dundee, Scotland, standing outside the mansion's service entrance, ca. 1926. She began to work for the Carnegies first at Skibo around 1911, when she was sixteen, eventually making the regular journeys between New York and Scotland with the family. She met her husband, a fellow Scot, in New York City, where he was working as a stonemason. Clarke left the Carnegies' employ sometime before the birth of her first child in 1930, to settle back in Scotland.

		Name	Relation			Age	Birthplace		Cit.	Occupation		
13	7	Burden, Jas A	Head	W	M	35	United States		Cit	Banker	Emp	
14		—, Florence	Wife	W	F	33	United States		Cit	×	×	
15		—, Jas. 3d	Son	W	M	9	United States		Cit	At School (9)	×	Block B.
16		—, William	Son	W	M	7	United States		Cit	At School (9)	×	begins
17		—, Florence	Daughter	W	F	3	United States		Cit	At Home	×	
18		Snell, Bertha	Servant	W	F	37	Sweden	10	Cit	Servant	W	
19		Anderson, Alma	Servant	W	F	28	Sweden	1	Al	Servant	W	
20	2	Carnegie, Andrew	Head	W	M	69	Scotland	61	Cit	Retired	Emp	
21		—, Louise	Wife	W	F	45	United States		Cit	×	×	
22		—, Margaret	Daughter	W	F	8	United States		Cit	At School (9)	×	
23		Steinhardt, Louis	Caretaker	W	M	50	Germany	30	Cit	Caretaker	W	
24		—, Lena	Servant	W	F	40	Germany	30	Cit	Servant	W	
25		Nichols, Elias	Servant	W	F	55	Scotland	1	Al	Servant	W	
26		Hughes, Agnes	Servant	W	F	35	Scotland	2	Al	Servant	W	
27		Cummings, Bessie	Servant	W	F	22	Scotland	1	Al	Servant	W	
28		Anderson, Maggie	Servant	W	F	35	Scotland	1	Al	Servant	W	
29		Stewart, Maggie	Servant	W	F	22	Scotland	1	Al	Servant	W	
30		Forsythe, Annie	Servant	W	F	25	Scotland	1	Al	Servant	W	
31		Forsythe, Maggie	Servant	W	F	23	Scotland	1	Al	Servant	W	
32		Elliott, Jane	Servant	W	F	25	Scotland	1	Al	Servant	W	
33		Forbes, Jeanette	Servant	W	F	25	Scotland	1	Al	Servant	W	
34		McKenzie, Elias	Servant	W	F	40	Scotland	1	Al	Servant	W	
35		Irving, George	Servant	W	M	50	Scotland	1	Al	Servant	W	
36		Duncan, Robert	Servant	W	M	22	Scotland	1	Al	Servant	W	
37		Watson, Thomas	Servant	W	M	23	Scotland	1	Al	Servant	W	
38		Bellview, William	Servant	W	M	25	Scotland	1	Al	Servant	W	
39	22	Butler, Howard	Head	W	M	49	United States		Cit	Artist	Emp	
40		—, Virginia	Wife	W	F	39	United States		Cit	×	×	
41		—, Howard, Jr	Son	W	M	9	United States		Cit	At School (9)	×	
42		McCrackin, Bridget	Servant	W	F	48	Ireland	18	Cit	Servant	W	
43		Beatty, Elizabeth	Servant	W	F	22	Ireland	7	Cit	Servant	W	
44		Doyle, Nellie	Servant	W	F	25	Ireland	10	Cit	Servant	W	
45	48	Wyman, Mary	Head	W	F	54	United States		Cit	×	×	
46		Hilman, Max	Son-in-Law	W	M	36	United States		Cit	Wholesale Butcher	Emp	
47		—, Eulalia	Daughter	W	F	29	United States		Cit	×	×	
48		—, Evard	Grandchild	W	M	7	United States		Cit	At School (9)	×	
49		Hillbroy, Harry	Son-in-Law	W	M	37	United States		Cit	Manufacturer	Emp	
50		—, Maud	Daughter	W	F	25	United States		Cit	×	×	

The New York State census of 1910, listing the Carnegies and their servants residing at 2 East 91st Street. Next door at 22 East 91st Street are Howard Russell Butler and his family.

or inn. The party was held in the servants' hall on the ground floor and was attended by Mr. and Mrs. Carnegie, Margaret, and Stella Whitfield. The family stayed for three dances, with Margaret ("the idol of the servants' hall") and Aunt Stella dancing each one, "to the delight of all."

A typical mansion in the Gilded Age included a butler and underbutler, several footmen, the head housekeeper, a lady's maid, a nursery governess, additional chambermaids and laundresses, a cook or two and an assistant, electrical engineers to manage the house's lighting and heating, workmen to shovel snow, carry coal, and do other work, a private watchman, stable hands for the horses and carriages, and in the garage, chauffeurs and assistants.

The Carnegies had this complement of help; they also each had secretaries—James Bertram and his staff of assistants for Andrew, and for Louise, Archibald Barrow, who worked for her for forty-six years. In addition to the live-in help, the Carnegies also had their hired musicians—Angus MacPherson, the piper, and Walter Gale, the organist—and an external hired security force. Although the house was enclosed by a tall iron fence and large urn-capped stone pillars, Carnegie was such a public figure that the house was the site of frequent attempted break-ins. In 1912 a "tall, swarthy"

former farmer from Minnesota lingered outside the mansion for days before he finally succeeded in scaling the fence, at which point "he was captured by a private watchman and ejected." In 1915, at a time of heightened unrest and anarchist activity, George Malone of the Holmes Electric Protective Company was patrolling the perimeter of the mansion while the Carnegies were away in Bar Harbor, Maine. During one of his regular passes, made each half hour, he spied "the sputter of a flame in the darkness" and discovered a crudely made dynamite bomb, which he managed to extinguish.

Many of the servants can be documented through census records, which list the names and ages and places of origin for all those living at 2 East 91st Street. But perhaps because the staff was so often in transit between Scotland and New York, there are a number of servants who never appeared in the records. Some are known from newspaper articles, such as the 1917 account of a flash fire in the Carnegie kitchen, which burned Vera Swanson, a twenty-four-year-old cook, "so severely, that her life is despaired of." The article also mentioned an electrical engineer not in the census records, William Gilliland, who was injured in his efforts to save Swanson. And Cooper Hewitt learned of Martha "Mattie" Clarke's service when her great-grandson contacted the museum.

The kitchen, seen here in 1938, featured an enormous electric range containing ten burners, all providing different levels of heat, each controlled by a separate switch, as well as electric ovens, a roaster, and a broiler. The food was prepared here and delivered to the butler's pantry upstairs by means of an electric dumbwaiter.

BASEMENT

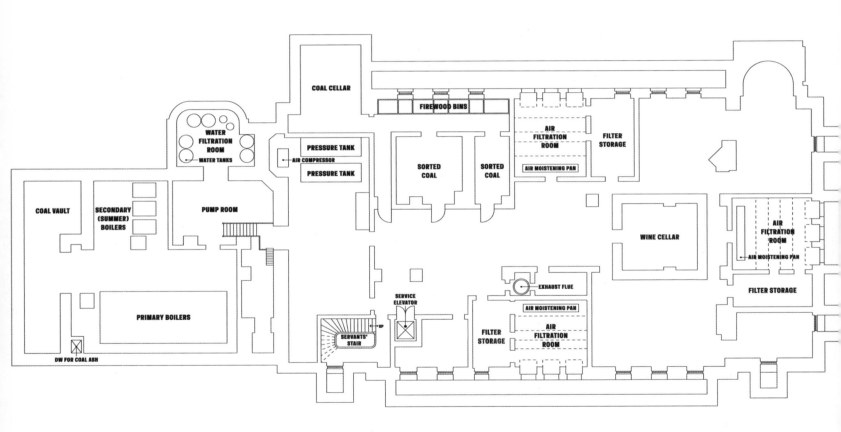

COAL CELLAR

FIREWOOD BINS

WATER
FILTRATION
ROOM

WATER TANKS

PRESSURE TANK

AIR COMPRESSOR

PRESSURE TANK

SORTED
COAL

SORTED
COAL

AIR
FILTRATION
ROOM

FILTER
STORAGE

AIR MOISTENING PAN

COAL VAULT

SECONDARY
(SUMMER)
BOILERS

PUMP ROOM

WINE CELLAR

AIR
FILTRATION
ROOM

AIR MOISTENING PAN

FILTER STORAGE

EXHAUST FLUE

SERVICE
ELEVATOR

PRIMARY BOILERS

UP

SERVANTS'
STAIR

DW FOR COAL ASH

AIR MOISTENING PAN

FILTER
STORAGE

AIR
FILTRATION
ROOM

The basement, below the ground floor, was the realm of the engineers. It contained the house's mechanical, electrical, and plumbing departments. Entering it was like arriving in the bowels of a great ocean liner. "At first glimpse we felt a kind of awe," wrote the author of a profile of the house in *Domestic Engineering* magazine in 1910. "This engineering department looks to us as if giants (truly of brain) had built it and equipped it—and the fairies had whisked in to finish it." Alexander Morrison, who joined the staff in 1905, could not remember Carnegie ever visiting the basement of the house. There was plenty here, however, that would have delighted the old man, and no doubt he made a keen inspection when the house was first completed.

The centerpiece of the boiler room was the immense twin boilers. The room was tiled with white glazed brick, and the corners of the room were rounded, to prevent dust from accumulating. The floor featured train tracks and a turntable, to facilitate passage of the railroad car that carried the coal from the enormous coal chutes, which held up to 200 tons of coal, at the eastern end of the building. The little railroad car, which transported the coal to the boilers, could carry three-quarters of a ton of coal, and on a cold winter's day it required two trips—one and a half tons of coal—to keep the house warm.

The mansion had a remarkably sophisticated system for heating and ventilating the house. Attic fans pulled the air for the house in through windows at the basement level into three enormous filtering chambers. Ten-foot-high filters removed impurities from the air, before it passed through a tempering chamber, over heating coils calibrated to heat the air to about 65 degrees. The air then passed over copper air-moistening pans. The cleansed, tempered, and moistened air was then ready for delivery upstairs, either as simple ventilation or passed through stacks to heat it further to the required temperature. Each room on the principal floors had an individual thermostat, which controlled a double damper, allowing the room's occupant to choose humidified air that was heated or not. Hung near the chambers at the west end of the basement was a hygrophant—a newly invented instrument for determining relative humidity.

The water supply to the house was also state-of-the-art. All the water that entered the house, drawn from two separate street mains, was purified. It passed through sand filters—large vertical cast-iron cylinders, one filled with crushed quartz and the other with high-quality bone char—used in tandem. The water for domestic purposes, used for feeding the steam-heating boilers and the fire service, bathing, washing, and other household chores, as well as sprinkling the lawn and garden, was then directed to the pump room, where it could be heated if needed and pumped through the rest of the house.

The water for drinking purposes went through yet another filtering process, passing through German earthenware filtering tubes made of "infusorial earth,"

The twin Babcock & Wilcox boilers, opposite, were each capable of carrying 200 pounds of steam pressure. Carnegie ordered doubles of all systems to provide backup or auxiliary service. Cast-iron hot-water boilers, at right, made up a separate system for heating the conservatory and the gardener's cellar underneath it. A steam boiler was used in the summer for the hot-water heater and the laundry service, when the family was in Scotland and the main boilers were shut down.

One of the house's engineers in the sixteen-foot-high pump room in the subbasement, where the walls were lined with glazed brick, in 1910. The machine pumps, which directed the water through the house and also into the sewer, were all worked by electricity.

OPPOSITE Floor detail, glazed tile.

so fine they were said to remove typhoid or cholera bacilli. This potable water was then carried through the house to the rooms specially equipped with drinking-water faucets.

The basement served many more purposes, however, than just housing the services of the mansion. The female servants, whom Carnegie did not permit to go out at night, were allowed to roller-skate in the basement for entertainment. The basement storage areas also contained large piles of gifts.

According to one newspaper article, "soft knit bedroom slippers, the shawls, and curious carved walking sticks" were some of the many presents that flooded Carnegie's mail delivery. Most of these gifts appeared with no card, and so they were placed to one side, as sure enough, at some later point the donor would write inquiring about the reception of the gift and more often than not explain that he or she had since fallen on hard times. At that point, the gift would be bundled up with a form letter explaining that "Mr. Carnegie appreciates the feeling which prompted the gift, but he does not wish to deprive the giver of such a valuable thing, and therefore returns it."

The basement contained a large wine cellar, with terra-cotta racks for some three thousand bottles, built right into the walls. It too had its own thermostat control. There was also a seventy-five-gallon cask of Scotch whisky, which Carnegie had specially imported. According to Alexander Morrison, the house steward, Carnegie "took an occasional nip" of whisky but did not touch wine. Carnegie regularly presented bottles of Scotch whisky to his closest friends. Most of the correspondence from Samuel Clemens (Mark Twain) to Carnegie in fact details Clemens's gratitude at the latest shipment: "The whisky came at the right time. Of course—for whisky never comes at the wrong time." (While the whisky was Mr. Carnegie's special gift, Mrs. Carnegie's signature offering was Skibo oatmeal.)

In 1949, when the New York School of Social Work occupied the mansion, the wine cellar was empty, but it still bore little white cards inscribed "Marsala," "Sparkling Moselle," and so forth.

THE ELEVATOR

The Carnegie Mansion was technologically advanced as well in its use of elevators. Although some grand New York mansions had residential elevators at least as early as the late 1870s, these early instances were all hydraulic elevators. The Carnegie Mansion elevators, manufactured by Otis, were state-of-the-art, run on electricity. The house in fact boasted five elevators, though only two were designed to carry passengers. This electric Otis elevator, now in the Smithsonian's National Museum of American History, was the principal passenger elevator used to carry guests and family members through the house. The house's second elevator was Andrew Carnegie's private car, which took him from the front hall to the entrance to the family library, or teak room, on the second floor. The other three elevators facilitated the service functions of the mansion: to haul the ash from the furnaces out to the street level; to transport potted plants from the ground floor to the conservatory; and to act as the dumbwaiter, to send food from the kitchen up to the butler's pantry, for service to the dining room or breakfast room. Unlike the other electrical elevators, the dumbwaiter operated on a direct current rather than an alternating current and was said to have been one of the first examples of such an installation.

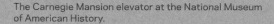

The Carnegie Mansion elevator at the National Museum of American History.

The skilit interior of the garage at 55 East 90th Street, with the chauffeurs showing off three cars.

The Carnegies' garage, located at 55 East 90th Street, a block east of the mansion's garden.

THE GARAGE

Some of the servants who did not live in the mansion had quarters a block away on 90th Street, on the two upper floors of the Carnegies' garage. The census of 1910 listed eight people living at this property, including a footman and four chauffeurs (all born in Scotland), and Kenneth Weatherbee, the superintendent of the garage, with his Scots-English wife.

Andrew Carnegie had commissioned his wife's architect brother, Henry Whitfield, to build this "automobile house" a few years after the family had moved into the mansion.

The garage housed the family's electric car, bought in the fall of 1904. (There was space in the garage in fact for five electric cars, and within a few years the family had acquired three.) Margaret, then seven years old, vividly remembered the afternoon she was told they were going for a drive in this new contraption, which "went by itself without horses": "'Will it go fast up the hills?' I asked. Horses walked so slowly up the hills pulling the carriage. It seemed as if it took forever. With Baxter sitting high up at the wheel, it did go fast up the hills in Central Park. What a thrill! It was terrific!"

The fireproof brick building, with white marble trim, had a large central bay flanked by two smaller entrances. On the right was a little office, containing the desk of the chauffeur on duty and the telephone alcove providing connection to the main house. On the

other side of the central bay was the entrance vestibule and stair to the upper floors. The garage's main floor was paved with white vitrified tiles, and the walls—like those in the basement at the mansion—were lined with semiglazed brick. Dividing the principal room from the charging station at the rear were a firewall and sliding door. All maintenance work on the vehicles was done in-house, so the charging room, which contained two battery-charging switchboards with rheostats, featured a working pit and a hydraulic lift. There was also a large elevator, which lifted the cars not in use up to a rear second-floor storage room. This room contained a third charging switchboard, adjacent to a washing stand where the cars were cleaned.

Whitfield was brought back in 1914 to add a fourth story to the building. By the 1950s, the garage was being used, in part, as an office for Margaret Carnegie Miller. In 1964 she sold it to the nursery school that had been operating in her former house. (Columbia University's School of Social Work, which had leased 9 East 90th Street to the nursery, wanted the Miller House for additional classroom space.) The nursery school renovated the garage building, retaining only the original ground-story elevation and expanding the building to six utilitarian stories. In 1969 they turned it over to Horace Mann, which still occupies the building for its nursery school.

Andrew Carnegie and his family were at Skibo in the late summer of 1914, when war was declared against Germany. The Liberal statesman Lord Morley resigned from the government and arrived at Skibo to find some solace with his old peace-loving friend a week later. Horses and equipment from the estate were all being requisitioned, and the family watched as a steady stream of the young men of their staff headed off to war. When the Carnegies left for home, on a ship painted gray, with the windows all blacked out, they little suspected it would be the last time that Andrew Carnegie would ever see Scotland.

For a man who had devoted much of his life and fortune to lobbying for peace, the advent of war was very distressing. "All my air castles," he told a friend, "have crashed about me like a house of cards." Carnegie was nevertheless fundamentally an optimist at heart, and he continued to hold out hope that America would find a way to put an end to the war. A year into the war, however, this intensely active eighty-year-old man, who had never been much of a brooder, turned inward and retreated from society. He made one last public appearance, in 1915, testifying before the U.S. Congress's Commission on Industrial Relations, chaired by Kansas City attorney and reformer Frank P. Walsh, on philanthropic bodies created by men of wealth. The *New York Times* reported that he captivated the commission "by the sheer force of his infectious geniality, . . . and had the crowd in roars of laughter."

But the exertion and excitement of the event, followed by a case of the flu, seem to have caused something of a breakdown. Carnegie's last few years were quiet and withdrawn. The 1892 Homestead strike—the loss of life and the criticism that came his way afterward—continued to dog his conscience. He often also thought of his mother. In April 1919, on his wedding anniversary, he celebrated his daughter's marriage at the mansion, accompanying her down the stairs to organ music. A few months later, on August 22, when he and his wife were summering at Shadow Brook, the massive house in Lenox, Massachusetts, that they had purchased when the war prevented them from going to Skibo, Carnegie caught pneumonia. Within a few days he was dead.

Carnegie, toward the end of his life.

THE MANSION AFTER CARNEGIE

In the fall of 1919 Mrs. Carnegie returned to 2 East 91st Street, where she would continue to live, with fourteen servants, for the rest of her life. In the course of just a few months, she had lost both her daughter, who was now married and living in her own house, and her husband.

She sold Shadow Brook to the Jesuits of the New England Province. She hoped very much to be able to maintain Skibo Castle as a gathering place. In 1920 Margaret gave birth to her first child, named Louise after Mrs. Carnegie, in her old room at 2 East 91st Street, while her mother and husband waited in Mrs. Carnegie's sitting room nearby. The year 1920 marked the first summer that they were able to return to Scotland after the long hiatus caused by World War I and Carnegie's illness. Happily, for this new start, there was a newborn, just as there had been in 1898, their first year at Skibo.

Although she had always had a firm, quiet hand in directing the affairs at 2 East 91st Street, it was only after Carnegie's death that Louise began to shape the neighborhood around the mansion. In 1924 she sold the property along Fifth Avenue to the south of the house, which Carnegie had bought in 1917 to protect the open space of the garden, to the Episcopal Church of the Heavenly Rest. In 1928 she gave 22 East 91st Street to the Spence School, Margaret's alma mater; the school hired architect John Russell Pope to design a new building for the site. For both of these building projects, Mrs. Carnegie retained final approval over the designs. She agreed to the sale to

Louise Carnegie in the drawing room, by Walter Scott Shinn.

Heavenly Rest on the condition that any church built on the site not exceed seventy-five feet in height, exclusive of any steeple. As it turned out, the building designed by Bertram Goodhue's successors was a streamlined Moderne neo-Gothic monolith with no steeple at all.

Most important, in 1920 she bought the town house at 9 East 90th Street, which abutted the garden, for her daughter Margaret's family. Margaret's four children would give Mrs. Carnegie a new lease on life following the loss of her husband, and she dedicated a part of the garden to them, covering it with boards and rubber and setting up a sandbox, jungle gym, and swings.

OPPOSITE Detail of the decorative ceiling in the library.

MILLER AND FOX HOUSES

The Miller House at 9 East 90th Street and the Fox House, next door at number 11, were built in 1902, just as the Carnegie Mansion was being completed. David McAlpin, who had made his fortune in tobacco, bought these lots in 1876—making him technically the first wealthy businessman to venture north of what was fashionable residential territory to this area. He originally built three houses on this land for his three sons. When he died in 1901, the family demolished the three houses and built these two larger row houses. George McAlpin and his family lived in number 9, a bowfront neo-Georgian house of redbrick and marble trim, designed by George Keister. William McAlpin's family occupied the adjacent number 11, designed by Barney and Chapman.

George McAlpin sold his house to Mrs. Carnegie in 1920, and it became the home of Margaret and Roswell and their growing family. They built a large addition in 1928, designed by Almus Pratt Evans, extending into the Carnegie garden and providing a new garden entrance for the house. After the death of Mrs. Carnegie, the house, along with the mansion, became the charge of Carnegie Corporation. The New York School of Social Work leased the house to a nursery school but then later used it for the school's research work.

The Arthur Ross Reading Room in the Smithsonian Design Library, 2012, in the former Fox House.

OPPOSITE Cooper Hewitt, Smithsonian Design Museum campus, with the Miller-Fox Houses in the foreground, 2007.

In 1917 Andrew Carnegie purchased the lot to the south of the garden, where a lemonade stand had stood for many years. Apartment buildings were beginning to spring up along Fifth Avenue, and Carnegie wished to prevent such a building from overshadowing his property. He let the land for playing tennis in the summer and ice-skating, as seen here, in the winter.

The two households maintained a constant back-and-forth. The children played in the garden regularly, with Margaret visiting her mother daily. Mrs. Carnegie continued to open the house and garden occasionally to the public for charity benefits. These became less frequent as she approached the end of her life, but the garden remained a great comfort to her in her last years. As her biographer wrote, "She took in its sun and air until she died, making note of the changes the seasons wrought, from the coloring by frost, and the snowfall covering the foliage with white beauty, to the coming of the first spring flowers and the blossoming of the dogwood and wisteria. On one of the days of her last springtime, she made note: 'Walked in garden; saw first robin.'" As her life wound down ("The time has come for the leaf to fall from the tree," she told her daughter), she spent almost every day sitting in the garden, taking in the birds and flowers of springtime.

THE MANSION AS SCHOOL

Louise Carnegie died June 24, 1946, at home at 2 East 91st Street, with her daughter by her bedside. She was eighty-nine and had been ill for the last year of her life. In her will, which she had drawn up three years earlier, she left the mansion to Carnegie Corporation of New York. The Spence School, her daughter's alma mater, was given the strip of land located between the school and the Carnegie property, in order "to assure light and air to the school."

Andrew Carnegie had ensured that his daughter was amply taken care of in his will, and while he wanted his wife as well to be secure, he had made clear early in their courtship that he intended to give away his millions. Mrs. Carnegie had in fact signed a kind of prenuptial agreement prior to their wedding. In light of the fact that her daughter was well established with her own family, it made sense that the mansion should become another asset for Carnegie Corporation to administer.

What, however, was Carnegie Corporation to do with the house? The foundation did not need it as office space. Since 1914 the foundation had been established at 576 Fifth Avenue. The house continued to be maintained by a staff of five, led by the Scots house steward Alexander Morrison, who had been with the Carnegies for more than forty years, while the foundation sought a use that would "carry on the Carnegie tradition." The foundation informally offered it as a "club and office" for the new United Nations—a fitting occupant, given Carnegie's pursuit of world peace—but nothing came of the proposal.

In 1949 Carnegie Corporation found an ideal tenant: the New York School of Social Work, affiliated with Columbia University. The school, which had coincidentally been established in 1898, the very year that the first plans for the Carnegie Mansion were sketched, enjoyed a wonderful heyday during its two decades at 2 East 91st Street.

Margaret Miller, with her husband, Roswell, standing behind her, hands over the key to the Carnegie Mansion to Bayard Pope, the president of the Community Service Society, the parent organization of the New York School of Social Work, with Charles Dolland, president of Carnegie Corporation, looking on, April 14, 1949.

To prepare the house for its new role, which would see bedrooms transformed into classrooms, and lounge and eating areas and restroom facilities for faculty and students carved out of the private family dwelling, the foundation engaged architect Edgar I. Williams, the brother of poet William Carlos Williams.

The old white-tiled kitchen of the ground floor was adapted for use as the cafeteria, and the servants' dining room was made into a students' lounge. On the main floor Carnegie's old library was made into the school's library, a transition that required hardly any change. The nearby drawing room, its elaborate gilded plasterwork left intact, was filled with shelving units and tables and made into a reading room, and Carnegie's secretary's room was turned into the stacks area. The large picture gallery at the building's east end was arranged for use as a lecture hall. Upstairs on the second floor, the Carnegies' private living quarters were turned into classrooms, and the spacious bathrooms with their silver-plated fixtures were filled with rows of bathroom stalls and sinks.

General Dwight D. Eisenhower, president of Columbia University, and other members of the administration celebrated the installation of a school dedicated to community service in the home of a man who gave his fortune to help others; they highlighted the motto in the library, "The

The Carnegies' dining room became the faculty lounge.

highest form of worship is service to man." But most students could not help but comment on the striking juxtaposition of their luxurious new academic setting and the focus of their studies and social work placements—"the cognitive dissonance," as one student recalled, "of the culture of social work being taught in a former bastion of industrial wealth." Nevertheless, the house and its garden offered "a fortress of peace from the outside realities." And the setting contributed greatly to the students' cohesiveness, inspiring them, as one student noted, to "preserve and transplant the 91st Street spirit into our current mission."

Carnegie Corporation of New York had given the school a rent-free, twenty-one-year lease, with an option to renew. In 1959 the school, which had become affiliated with Columbia in 1940, became an official academic faculty of the university. By that time outgrowing its home in the Carnegie Mansion, it began the search for new premises on the Morningside Heights campus. Although in the coming years the school initiated planning for a new campus building by Edward Durrell Stone, that project did not materialize, and instead Columbia renovated the Miller House at 9 East 90th Street and expanded into that property. The school relocated to Columbia's main campus at the end of the 1960s.

ABOVE Students smoking as Gardner Cook leads a seminar in the teak room.
RIGHT Carnegie's library in use by the New York School of Social Work.

THE MANSION AS MUSEUM

n 1963, the Cooper Union for the Advancement of Science and Art announced that it was disbanding its museum. Inventor and industrialist Peter Cooper, who believed that education lay at the heart of a healthy civic state, had established the school in 1859 to provide an institution of higher learning "open and free to all." Central to that mission had been the creation of a museum, which was accomplished through the efforts of his granddaughters, the Hewitt sisters, in 1897. For more than half a century, inspired by the Musée des Arts Décoratifs in Paris and the Victoria and Albert Museum in London, the museum amassed and organized its vast reference collections in ways conducive to exploration of, comparison of, and ongoing dialogue on decorative arts and design.

The looming dispersal of the Cooper Union Museum generated a tremendous outcry. Philanthropist Alice Kaplan, then president of the American Federation of Arts, established the Committee to Save the Cooper Union Museum in the living room of her Upper East Side town house—a committee, as she described it, that "was formed in outrage." Henry Francis du Pont, scion of the chemical company family, who had turned his Delaware estate Winterthur into one of the premier American decorative arts museums, served as chairman, despite being nearly ninety. Within a few months the group numbered more than 250 people. There were many Upper East Side

LEFT Tetrahedrons and octahedrons in Carnegie's library served as an entry to Buckminster Fuller's film exploring the "elegantly meshed design of the universe," part of *MAN transFORMs*—the inaugural exhibition in the Carnegie Mansion (October 7, 1976–February 7, 1977).
OPPOSITE Detail of one of the carved stone decorations on the exterior of the mansion.

The Hewitt sisters in a gondola in Venice, on one of their many collecting trips in Europe, ca. 1890.

THE COOPER UNION MUSEUM

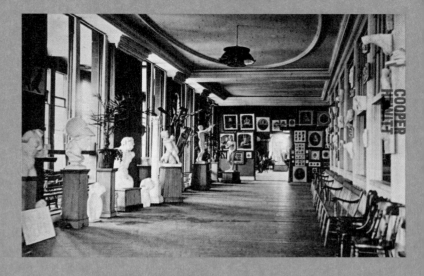

The Museum of Decorative Art was founded by Peter Cooper's granddaughters, in accordance with his larger aspirations for the Cooper Union, an institution he hoped would enrich the public both intellectually and morally. As part of the services offered by the school, Cooper envisioned a reading room accompanied by a gallery, and in his letter to the trustees of the Cooper Union in 1859, the year of its founding, he wrote, "And when a sufficient collection of the works of art, science, and nature can be obtained, I propose that glass cases shall be arranged around the walls of the gallery. . . . I propose to arrange such cosmoramic and other views as will exhibit in the clearest and most forcible light the true philosophy of life." What he imagined was not a traditional collection of fine art, but rather a collection of decorative arts and material culture displayed with the explicit purpose of teaching. This is precisely the vision carried out by the Misses Hewitt for the museum that officially opened at the Cooper Union in 1897.

Beginning very early in their lives, Amy, Sarah, and Eleanor Hewitt amassed a large collection of decorative arts. The creation of the museum was meant to supplement the education of the students in the art schools, specifically the Women's Art School, which was championed by the sisters, who sat on the Ladies Advisory Council and oversaw many of the art school's functions. The museum also served as a resource for designers and artisans in the community. It encompassed architectural decoration, birdcages, buttons, costume accessories, decorative paintings, designs, drawings, embroidery, engravings and etchings, books on flowers and horticulture, furniture glass, Japanese sword mountings, jewelry, lace, metalwork, porcelain, pottery, straw work, textiles, tiles, toys and games, wallpaper and bandboxes, woodwork, and works by American artists. The collection was meant to be used in conjunction with the library, which boasted a large collection of reference books and art periodicals, as well as unique "Encyclopedic Scrap Books" Eleanor Hewitt had created. The result was very much an expansive, accessible, living, breathing, working collection—one that, in Eleanor's words, was "formed to facilitate the free acquisition of knowledge in the arts, styles, and periods."

ABOVE A view of the museum, which opened on the fourth floor of the Cooper Union in 1897. The plaster cast collection, some of which had been given by the Musée des Arts Décoratifs in Paris, was an important aspect of the learning collection.

ANDREW CARNEGIE AND THE COOPER AND HEWITT FAMILIES

The paths of the philanthropic steel men Andrew Carnegie and Peter Cooper, and those of Abram Hewitt and Cooper's Hewitt descendants, crossed long before their posthumous collaboration began with the creation and installment of the Smithsonian's Cooper-Hewitt Museum in the Carnegie Mansion in the 1970s.

Peter Cooper (1791–1883) was a New York–born inventor and industrialist who became one of the richest men in mid-nineteenth-century Manhattan, and late in life, at age eighty-five, became the oldest nominated candidate for president of the United States. He was famous for having designed and built the first steam locomotive in America, and he made his fortune in iron-works for the railroad, though he also invested in real estate. A fervent abolitionist and supporter of the Union, he was active in Native American rights and in the cause of public education. In 1859 he founded the Cooper Union for the Advancement of Science and Art in Manhattan, which offered free practical education in the arts and sciences to workingmen and women. It was Peter Cooper's ambitious approach to philanthropy and his championing of the public good that spurred other members of the elite like Andrew Carnegie to disperse their wealth back into the community.

Carnegie and Cooper's shared sense of social responsibility was manifest in Carnegie's continued support of the Cooper Union, even long after Peter Cooper's death. He served as a trustee for many years,

Peter Cooper, ca. 1870s.

often alongside Cooper's son-in-law Abram S. Hewitt (1822–1903), the mayor of New York City, and also gave a large gift that alleviated the organization's debt. At a meeting held in tribute for Cooper, Carnegie said that Cooper "found his mission among people of his own class, and therefore pointed the way which millionaires the world over should follow—that is, the possessor of surplus wealth should distribute it for the benefit of those who helped to accumulate it."

Carnegie was friends as well with Abram Hewitt, who married Sarah Amelia Cooper, having already become practically a member of the family through his close friendship with Peter Cooper's other surviving child, Edward. In addition to detailing their business dealings and shared interest in the Cooper Union, correspondence between Carnegie and Hewitt offers glimpses of planned encounters between the two families at Skibo Castle, Hewitt's Ringwood Manor in New Jersey, and other summer homes. Hewitt became a founding trustee of the Carnegie Institution in Washington, D.C., and he also gave Carnegie land for his libraries in New York City. Hewitt admired Carnegie's philanthropy, since libraries, like the Cooper Union, were also for the betterment of the public. In a tribute to Hewitt, Carnegie called him "America's foremost private citizen," and at one time Hewitt named Carnegie "the 'Grand Old Man' of the United States, honest, pure, exceeding[ly] wise, public-spirited, and patriotic."

In 1903, Abram Hewitt passed away, and Carnegie acted as a pallbearer at Abram's funeral alongside J. P. Morgan and John E. Parsons. The Cooper Union's annual report of that year published Andrew Carnegie's remarks praising Hewitt's life and works, especially his work at the Cooper Union. When, the following year, the Hewitt Memorial Endowment was set up in Abram's name, Carnegie gave the greatest sum, $55,000.

Peter Cooper, Abram Hewitt, and Andrew Carnegie were bound under the common belief that with great wealth comes great social responsibility. Not unlike the descendants and family members of Peter Cooper, including Amy, Sarah, and Eleanor Hewitt and many others, who were known to have given up their inheritances to bolster the school's endowment, Carnegie gave generously to Cooper Union as well as to his own causes in an effort to follow Cooper's legacy. At the celebration of Founders Day in 1909, which marked the 118th anniversary of Peter Cooper's birth, Carnegie, who was sitting next to one of Cooper's granddaughters and founders of the museum, said of Cooper to the attendees, "'He was my great exemplar, one in whose footsteps I humbly try to tread.'"

stalwarts, arts philanthropists, and design scholars and practitioners involved: Mrs. Robert Woods (Mildred Barnes) Bliss, who had given her Georgetown estate, Dumbarton Oaks, to Harvard University in 1940 to found a museum and research center dedicated to Byzantine and pre-Columbian art and archeology; Mrs. Roger Brunschwig, the design director of the textile company Brunschwig & Fils; Edith Gregor Halpert, founder of Downtown Gallery in Greenwich Village and champion of American modernists such as Georgia O'Keeffe and Stuart Davis; art history scholars H. W. Janson and Erwin Panofsky; notable architect Ely Jacques Kahn; architect Edgar Kauffman Jr., whose father had commissioned Frank Lloyd Wright to build Fallingwater; Lincoln Kirstein, New York culture broker and founder of the New York Ballet; famed architectural critic Lewis Mumford; decorator-socialite Sister Parish (née Dorothy May Kinnicutt); Pulitzer Prize–winning author Margaret Leech (Mrs. Ralph Pulitzer); Henry Hope Reed, architectural critic and avid antimodernist; Francis Steegmuller, devoted biographer of Flaubert; and philanthropist and drawings collector Eugene V. Thaw among them.

As the critic Ada Louise Huxtable so aptly described it, "The museum was disowned and faced with dismemberment by a financially hard-pressed Cooper Union, whose architecture students were more involved with urban problems than ormolu." She called the situation a "cultural cliff-hanger." For a while, it seemed likely that the collection would be dispersed, sold at auction, or taken by the Metropolitan Museum of Art—a solution that would have sent much of the collection into storage, never to be seen. Over four years the beleaguered curatorial staff of the museum and the committee to save the museum worked to preserve the collection intact and find a new home. Du Pont facilitated the development of a relationship with the Smithsonian. With an endorsement from the American Association of Museums, the Smithsonian agreed in 1967 to make the newly named Cooper-Hewitt Museum part of the national collections.

Carnegie Corporation of New York came forward with the offer of a home for this new entity: the Carnegie Mansion, which was being vacated by the School of Social Work in 1969. Initially the foundation leased the building to the Smithsonian for $1 a year, with an option to purchase. When it proved difficult for the museum to fundraise for what seemed with the lease to be a temporary solution, the foundation decided instead in 1972 to give the house—then valued at about $8 million—outright.

For the Smithsonian, it was an adventure. Cooper-Hewitt represented the institution's first museum outside of Washington, D.C. It also soon became the first Smithsonian museum to be led by a woman. In 1969, Secretary of the Smithsonian S. Dillon Ripley appointed Lisa Taylor as director; until that time she had been in charge of the Smithsonian Associates, a new organization dedicated to building public programming for the institution. When

she arrived in New York, she was the only female director of a museum in the city.

The move into the historic Carnegie Mansion was part of an expansion boom for the Smithsonian. The Smithsonian had encompassed four museums for most of the first half of the twentieth century. Beginning in the 1960s, it opened new facilities and, by the time Cooper-Hewitt opened in 1976, it extended to ten museums. The Carnegie Mansion home also represented a new trend for the Smithsonian—the preservation and reopening to the public of landmark historic buildings. In Washington, the institution had recently opened the National Portrait Gallery and the National Collection of Fine Arts (today the Smithsonian American Art Museum) in the historic Greek Revival–style Patent Office Building (today the Donald W. Reynolds Center for American Art and Portraiture).

Cooper-Hewitt's new director, Lisa Taylor, recognized this zeitgeist. "We brought several contemporary architects through the Carnegie Mansion, only for them to tell us that it could never house a collection such as ours," she said. "But simultaneous with our decision to use the mansion anyway was the growth of public realization that our natural resources are limited. The use of an old building for a modern purpose is the essence of urban recycling, so I'm pleased to announce that . . . we have a museum that exemplifies in its facilities the very principles we are trying to communicate through our collections."

Lisa Taylor on the grand stair of the Carnegie Mansion in 1976, with a display of flags from the inaugural exhibition *MAN transFORMs*. The first director of Cooper-Hewitt, she retired in 1987.

ENTRANCE HALL
FIRST FLOOR

Hardy Holzman Pfeiffer's rendering of the museum's entrance hall.

The Smithsonian hired Hugh Hardy of Hardy Holzman Pfeiffer, a firm that specialized in the renovation of historic buildings, to adapt the mansion for use as a museum. "The first floor was so encrusted with history," according to Hardy, "that you really couldn't imagine wiping all that out." They restored the principal historic rooms on this main floor, while trying to make them suitable for exhibition use. Other areas were adapted to provide more contemporary gallery space. Hardy explained, "It was fun to figure out how to, on the second floor, be able to open the place up, and provide something like a series of galleries." The rooms along the south facade that once housed the sitting rooms of mother and daughter Carnegie had their dividing walls and their plaster ceilings removed to expose the building's basic structure.

Some of the third-floor historic fabric and floor plan was retained when the space was adapted for a library and study center, the Doris and Henry Dreyfuss Study

Hardy Holzman Pfeiffer's rendering of the third-floor library. The original long central hallway of the third floor functioned as the reading room, while the rooms around the perimeter served as offices and library collections storage.

STRUCTURAL STEEL

Carnegie was a passionate believer in fireproof construction, and the mansion was built using the latest such technology: the Roebling system of fireproof construction, developed at the end of the nineteenth century by John A. Roebling's Sons Company, the family who designed the Brooklyn Bridge. The rooms are spanned by riveted, built-up, steel I beams—made of course by Carnegie Steel—with the spaces between filled with shallow concrete vaulting. The arched vaults were formed using the company's special wire cloth made of woven-in steel rods. The result, the company boasted, was "a pleasing monolithic construction, admirably adapted for a fire-proof floor."

Steel I beam from the Carnegie Mansion, showing the Carnegie Steel imprint, exposed during the recent renovation, 2013.

The 1970s renovation of the mansion opened up the south side of the second floor, exposing the mansion's steel beam and shallow concrete vault construction and creating a long, open gallery space. In 2005, it held the "Tumbleweed" inflatable rover for exploring the surface of Mars, as part of the exhibition *Extreme Textiles: Designing for High Performance*. Developed at the Jet Propulsion Laboratory, the nylon airbag represented the latest in biologically inspired engineering.

Center. The ceiling, which once contained a stained-glass laylight, had been replaced in the New York School of Social Work renovations of the late 1940s. Renovating the top floor proved more challenging, because Carnegie had not extended the sophisticated heating and ventilation system that the main floors enjoyed to the servants' quarters. The partitions making up the servants' quarters were all demolished, and the floor reorganized to house a collection storage area and working space for the Drawings and Prints and for the Textiles departments.

One of the most critical problems to address was the increased circulation the museum would attract and the safety of these new visitors. The original circulation patterns of the mansion had been shaped by the family-servant dynamic. Now the building needed new vertical cores, to accommodate both the visiting public and new mechanical systems. Although the museum briefly considered retaining the Aeolian organ, the space it occupied represented one of the only large open shafts in the building, running from the basement to the third floor—an ideal space for a large elevator. A new fire stair was created by removing Carnegie's secretary's study on the north side of the building and Carnegie's bathroom above it. The servants' stair hall provided an excellent second fire stair.

COOPER-HEWITT OPENS TO THE PUBLIC

The museum opened in 1976, America's bicentennial year, on October 7, with tremendous fanfare. Around the city, other museums hosted *Salutes to the New Museum*, small satellite exhibitions of loans from Cooper-Hewitt that interacted with their own collections: drawings at the Morgan Library, rare natural history books at the American Museum of Natural History, painters' sketchbooks at the Whitney, and more.

The opening exhibition at the Carnegie Mansion was not a selection of highlights from the permanent collection, but instead what director Lisa Taylor billed "a very shocking show," entitled *MAN transFORMs*. The museum invited Austrian artist-architect Hans Hollein to curate the show, which featured contributions from international designers such as Buckminster Fuller, Richard Meier, George Nelson, Ettore Sottsass, Arata Isozaki, and others. *MAN transFORMs* emphasized the role that design has played in human history, affecting even the most elemental and basic aspects of our lives. Every space over three floors of the mansion was treated like an installation. One room featured an array of birdcages from varied periods and locales; another room displayed an enormous table filled with different kinds of breads made all over the world. "The objective," according to Hollein, "was to produce a series of encounters that would unfetter the imagination."

Taylor brought a playful, energetic program to the mansion. Nothing was off-limits, recalled former curator of exhibitions Dorothy Twining Globus: "shopping bags, lace, ocean liners, writing and reading, soup tureens and mustard pots, Antonio Gaudi, Robert Adam, the Royal Pavilion at Brighton, Mad King Ludwig," and more. The public came to expect the unexpected.

In 1978 the Samuel H. Kress Foundation funded the creation of a textile conservation laboratory, which was established on the ground floor in the former kitchen area of the mansion. Soon after, a paper conservation laboratory was added in an adjacent room. Lisa Taylor took care, as well, to ensure the future stewardship of Cooper-Hewitt and other museums by founding a master's program in decorative arts to train future curators. She also excelled at inserting Cooper-Hewitt into the cultural life of New York. Taylor dreamed up the idea of an annual Museum Mile open house festival on Upper Fifth Avenue, which was first held in 1978 and still thrives today.

Taylor retired in 1987 and was followed by Dianne Pilgrim, then chair of the Decorative Arts Department at the Brooklyn Museum. Pilgrim led the museum for more than a decade, during which time she focused on making the collection more accessible, both conceptually, in terms of broadening what fell under the definition of design, and physically, in transforming the mansion campus.

The mansion posed many challenges as a museum. It was a difficult environment for exhibitions. As former curator David McFadden recalled, "The house had such a big presence. The more you fought it, the more it disagreed with you." Lisa Taylor said much the same in an interview

RIGHT A racing dinghy and high-performance sail in the conservatory for *Extreme Textiles: Design for High Performance* (April 8–October 30, 2005), an exhibition exploring recent innovations in technical performance textiles.

RIGHT ABOVE *Andrea Palladio in America* (June 7–August 5, 1977) featured large wooden scale models of Palladio's villas and churches, and photographs of important American buildings influenced by the Italian sixteenth-century architect.

RIGHT BELOW John Lennon's yellow Rolls-Royce greeted visitors in the front entrance hall for the exhibition *Ornament in the Twentieth Century* (September 19–November 5, 1978).

in 1986: "It is a very strong building, and there's a constant struggle—how to make objects look good without destroying the building." The mansion's layout also complicated the staff's behind-the-scenes work. Large objects had to be brought in via the front door, necessitating the closure of the museum to the public whenever an exhibition was being installed or taken down. There was no easy means of communication between the offices and collection storage on 90th Street and the museum itself.

For years Pilgrim, who has multiple sclerosis and uses a wheelchair, had to enter the building via a service entrance, a process that required assistance. Under her leadership, the museum undertook an award-winning renovation, by Polshek and Partners Architects (today Ennead Architects), to make the building and the multi-level terraced garden fully accessible. Begun soon after

Dianne Pilgrim was Cooper-Hewitt's second director, from 1988 to 2000.

RIGHT *La Nijinska, A Dancer's Legacy* (March 18–July 6, 1986), an exhibition that traced the career of pioneering Modernist choreographer Bronislava Nijinska.

The conservatory showcased a large copper still from the Cognac region of France for *Wine: Celebration and Ceremony* (June 4–October 13, 1985).

ABOVE *L'Art de Vivre: Decorative Arts and Design in France, 1789–1989*, was a major exhibition held in 1989, at the time of France's bicentennial. Mrs. Carnegie's bedroom was overtaken by a model of the prow of the *Normandie*, the great Art Deco ocean liner.

OPPOSITE *Mixing Messages: Graphic Design in Contemporary Culture* (September 17, 1996–February 16, 1997) was the opening exhibition following the Polshek and Partners renovation.

LEFT Carnegie's library and office became the gift shop after the Polshek and Partners renovation, depicted here in 2004.

The Agnes Bourne Bridge Gallery, shown here in 1997.

the passage of the Americans with Disabilities Act (1990), the project turned the museum—once called "formidably inaccessible"—into a showcase for how to achieve accessibility in a historic building.

This work was part of a larger scheme Polshek and Partners was tasked with, to rethink the campus of the museum. Cooper-Hewitt had in 1989 acquired the Fox House, adjacent to the Miller House on 90th Street; the new master plan combined the two town houses, transforming them into a Design Resource Center dedicated to the care and study of the collections. The town houses were joined to the Carnegie Mansion with an elegant, two-story, pergola-inspired connector, the Agnes Bourne Bridge Gallery. Conceived initially as a gallery space, it subsequently became part of the café. These three disparate properties were now united into one complex, and a new mechanical plant was created to service the whole

campus. The project also entailed restoring the conservatory, renovating the mansion's first- and second-floor galleries, expanding the south gallery on the second floor, creating a new gift shop, and introducing new lighting throughout the museum. This work facilitated access to the collections, for both researchers and the general public; it also ensured a stable environment for the safeguarding of the collections for future generations.

In 1998 Polshek and Partners was brought in once more to renovate the mansion's fourth floor for the Drawings and Prints department. Two new study centers—the Drue Heinz Study Center for Drawings and Prints and the Henry Luce Study Room for American Art—were created. Visual and spatial fluidity, natural light, transparency, color, and materials were used to reinforce the inner workings of the department and to define its public identity. The two primary public spaces were separated only by a transparent pane of floor-to-ceiling glass, in order to expand the sense of space on the floor.

As Cooper-Hewitt approached the millennium, the museum launched several important initiatives. The annual National Design Awards—to honor lasting achievement in American design and to celebrate "excellence, innovation, and the enhancement of the quality of life"—quickly became a landmark event in the calendar of the design community. The National Design Triennial, created to provide a critical survey of the latest trends in American design, also began in 2000—with a show of eighty-three

U.S.-based designers, both established and emerging. It has since grown to encompass a global focus, showcasing design solutions from around the world focused on sustainability, social equity, accessibility, and creative capital.

In 2000 Paul Thompson, then director of Design Museum London, was named the museum's third director. Feeling that "the institution need[ed] to be revivified," in 2001 he hired Caroline Baumann as his Deputy Director, and together they initiated sweeping changes and embarked upon an ambitious plan to renovate and expand the museum campus. Thompson also focused new attention on the permanent collection, dedicating one room in the mansion, the Nancy and Edwin Marks Gallery, to its display and inaugurating an exhibition series in 2003 that invited prominent designers, artists, and authors to curate a selection of objects from the permanent collection that intrigue and inspire their own work. He oversaw the creation of the Target National Design Education Center on the ground floor of the museum, and in 2006, the museum launched National Design Week, to celebrate the role that design plays in daily life.

Thompson's major legacy was to initiate the renovation project transforming the museum campus. He sought to expand the public exhibition space in the museum, creating a contemporary white-box space in the mansion that had always been lacking. The project ultimately involved a complete renovation of the mansion and the two town houses.

Paul Thompson served as Cooper-Hewitt's third director, from 2001 to 2009.

The museum worked with the architectural firms Gluckman Mayner Architects and Beyer Blinder Belle Architects and Planners LLP as the design and executive architects for the renovation. The ambitious project had multiple aims: to restore the historically significant features inside and out of the landmarked mansion, to add operational efficiency by improving the art path and adding a large freight elevator, and most importantly to maximize the public space for design exhibitions.

In order to effect this transformation of the mansion, the functions of all the museum campus's spaces were reconceived. The design and construction plan entailed three sequential phases. In 2009, under direction of then Acting Director, Caroline Baumann the collections were moved from the town houses to a new off-site facility in New Jersey, designed to the highest preservation

OVERLEAF LEFT *Design for the Other 90%* (May 4–September 23, 2007) presented a variety of design solutions to address the basic needs and quality-of-life issues of the vast percentage of the world's population.

OVERLEAF RIGHT For the *National Design Triennial: Design Life Now* (December 8, 2006–July 29, 2007), landscape architect Ken Smith designed a large-scale flower scrim for the museum's front facade.

In 2009 Cooper-Hewitt opened a state-of-the-art off-site location in New Jersey. The building provides space for collections storage, study, digitization, and preservation. It also includes the museum's first object-conservation laboratory overseen by the museum's first objects conservator, a position made possible by a challenge endowment grant from the Andrew W. Mellon Foundation and the support of other donors. The Foundation also supported a conservation lab in the Miller-Fox Houses.

standards. The facility provides collections storage and conservation care, a study center for curators and visiting researchers, and a photography studio. Emptying the town houses of the collections freed the Miller and Fox Houses to be adapted for use as dedicated support buildings, housing offices, classrooms, and a new home for the museum's library. In 2011, the Smithsonian Design Library and staff offices moved from the mansion into the newly renovated Miller-Fox town house complex. With the offices and the library removed from the

Carnegie Mansion, that building could now be dedicated almost entirely to public use.

In 2010, Bill Moggridge, a cofounder of the renowned design firm IDEO and designer of the first laptop computer, became Cooper-Hewitt's fourth director. With plans for the comprehensive physical renovation of the museum campus already in place, Moggridge led a conceptual reimagining of the museum experience, work that he carried out together with his successor, Caroline Baumann. The aim for the museum was to move the visitor from observer to active participant. Moggridge selected Diller Scofidio + Renfro (National Design Award winner, 2005), the architectural design firm responsible for the reconceptualizing of Lincoln Center and the transformation of the derelict High Line into one of the most popular outdoor spaces in New York City, to help the staff plan the

Bill Moggridge became Cooper-Hewitt's fourth director in 2010, until his death in 2012.

Guest curators provided compelling new vantages on the collection. In *Yinka Shonibare Selects: Works from the Permanent Collection* (October 7, 2005–September 24, 2006), presented in the Nancy and Edwin Marks Gallery, the celebrated British-Nigerian artist mined the permanent collection—focusing in particular on the Hewitt sisters— to explore themes of imperialism, tourism, and cultural exchange.

visitor and gallery experience. Thinc Design was also hired to design the museum's major reopening exhibition, *Tools: Extending Our Reach*. Multimedia firm Local Projects (National Design Award winner, 2013) was invited to help conceive the participatory media design and to develop creative ways to digitally access the collection, both at the museum and remotely. "This project gave Cooper-Hewitt the opportunity to reinvent itself, to rethink museum conventions and the entire museum visit," Caroline Baumann explained.

Numerous spaces throughout the museum were named in recognition of donors' generosity. On the third floor of the mansion, the renovation resulted in the creation of the Barbara and Morton Mandel Design Gallery, and an expansive and versatile 6,000-square-foot

exhibition gallery—enabling the museum for the first time to mount large-scale design exhibitions in a contemporary space. The increased public exhibition area in the building also permits the museum to devote more space to displaying the rich permanent collection; the second-floor galleries are now dedicated to exhibitions drawn from the museum's core holdings. On the first floor, the relocation of the shop to the east end of the building, in the Lisa Roberts and David Seltzer Room, the former picture gallery, resulted in a more logical visitor-flow experience. In addition to the physical transformation, the museum changed its name to Cooper Hewitt, Smithsonian Design Museum, engaged Pentagram to design a new graphic identity, and adopted a new custom font, designed by Chester Jenkins of Village. The font "Cooper Hewitt" was donated to the

ABOVE Visitors to the new Cooper Hewitt encounter the Immersion Room, where they can interact with the collection.

ABOVE A rendering of the Agnes Bourne Bridge Gallery, home to relocated café seating.

COOPER-HEWITT BEYOND THE MANSION

With the closure of the museum in 2011 for renovation, Cooper-Hewitt was committed to continuing its exhibition and public programming activities by resourcefully collaborating with exciting partners around New York City, in a series of off-site venues. The museum opened a new design center in Harlem, the Cooper-Hewitt Design Center, with an interior designed by American designer Todd Oldham in collaboration with teens from the museum's DesignPrep program. Oldham envisioned it as "a street-level treehouse." Among the many events and workshops offered was a new Harlem Focus series, highlighting practitioners exploring design issues affecting the community.

Building on the museum's long-standing educational outreach, Cooper-Hewitt likewise instituted Design in the Classroom, sending design educators to public schools across New York City and nationally. To further extend the collection while it was closed during the renovation, the museum developed a series of traveling exhibitions to Europe and also for the first time to Asia, including an exhibition titled *Design with the Other 90%: Cities* at the United Nations, and a free summer-long exhibition in 2012, *Graphic Design—Now in Production* on Governors Island. The Enid and Lester Morse Historic Design Lecture series and a Design Talks series were both held off-site and webcast to the world.

Another significant outreach beyond the walls of the museum was a digital one. The museum's digital presence enables it to reach a global new audience and

Cooper-Hewitt's Harlem Design Center.

to open the collection to new kinds of research and use. In 2012 Cooper-Hewitt released a public prototype of its online collection database and became the first Smithsonian museum to release its descriptive text to the public domain. The online database with its iterative design approach permitted the public and the museum staff alike to see the totality of the collection rather than only small curated sections. The museum also started Object of the Day, offering original and personal stories about individual objects. The daily posts began a shift in how the museum communicated its knowledge to the public. In 2014 Cooper Hewitt embarked upon an ambitious mass digitization project aimed at photographing the entirety of the more than 200,000-object collection and building a firm foundation for future digital outreach.

LEFT The new Barbara and Morton Mandel Design Gallery on the third floor.
BELOW LEFT Barbara Mandel, Board Chair, and Caroline Baumann, Director, celebrating the completion of the Carnegie Mansion renovation in the Barbara and Morton Mandel Design Gallery.
BELOW RIGHT (RENDERING) The former picture gallery, now home to SHOP Cooper Hewitt in the Lisa Roberts and David Seltzer Room.

In 2013 Caroline Baumann, who had held a number of leadership positions since joining the museum in 2001, became the fifth director of Cooper-Hewitt.

museum's permanent collection and was released as a free download to the public.

The renovation included an important historic preservation component—from the complete restoration of the teak room to the exterior cleaning of the masonry and the refurbishment of the iron fence; the cleaning of the oak paneling on the main floors; the repair and cleaning of the Caen stone in the entry vestibule; and the replacement in matching teak of the patterned floorings of the first and second floors. The project also achieved LEED (Leadership in Energy and Environmental Design) certification.

Today the Carnegie Mansion is once again a technological marvel. This unique Gilded Age home has been restored and upgraded into a state-of-the-art museum. It features an integrated digital experience that in increasing the accessibility of the collection honors and celebrates the original mission of the Hewitt sisters when they assembled the collection, one that echoes as well the public mission of the Smithsonian's founding donor, James Smithson.

CARNEGIE MANSION NAMED SPACES

Agnes Bourne Bridge Gallery
Ainslie Family Gallery (former Garden Room)
Barbara and Morton Mandel Design Gallery (third floor)
Barbara Riley Levin Conservatory
Drue Heinz Study Center for Drawings and Prints (fourth floor)
Enid and Lester Morse Gallery (former Dining Room)
Henry Luce Study Room for American Art (fourth floor)
Krueger Family Grand Staircase in memory of Peter A. Krueger
Lisa Roberts and David Seltzer Room (former Picture Gallery)
Marks Family Gallery (Mrs. Carnegie's former Bedroom)
Nancy and Edwin Marks Gallery (former Music Room)
Spoon Family Gallery (hallway leading from former
    Picture Gallery to Main Hall)
Target National Design Education Center (ground floor)
Usdan Family Gallery (former Breakfast Room)

MILLER/FOX AND GARDEN NAMED SPACES

Arthur Ross Reading Room (second floor of Fox House)
Arthur Ross Terrace and Garden (Garden)
Di Palma Center for the Study of Jewelry and Precious Metals
    (fifth floor of Miller House)
Enid and Lester Morse Garden Room
Fred and Rae S. Friedman Rare Book Room
    (second floor of Miller House)
Nancy and Edwin Marks Master's Program Suite
    (sixth floor of Fox House)
Target Master's Program Students' Lounge
    (sixth floor of Fox House)

COOPER HEWITT'S GARDEN

In 1976, when Cooper-Hewitt opened, the Smithsonian had recently established a horticulture office. James Buckler, its founder and director, took a personal interest in this new addition to the Smithsonian family of gardens—but the distance from Washington meant that there was not much active development of the site. The garden, which had been much used by the neighborhood, consisted primarily of shrubs—the flower beds having fallen into disrepair. The spectacular historic wisteria climbing the facade remained, as did the rockery, many of the original trees, and the layout of the paths through the garden. The little summerhouse that had been built for Margaret's enjoyment also remained, for the first few years of the museum's existence at least.

In 1991, in recognition of a major gift from Arthur Ross, the garden became known as the Arthur Ross Terrace and Garden. Ross, an investment manager and philanthropist, had also underwritten research and development of an elm tree strain resistant to Dutch elm disease, and an example of an Arthur Ross Central Park elm now resides in the garden.

In 1992 Mary Riley Smith came to Cooper-Hewitt, at first in a volunteer capacity. She called on the well-known New York public garden designer Lynden Miller, director of the Conservatory Garden in Central Park, for help in selecting plants and making decisions. Together with a corps of volunteers from the Conservatory Garden, Riley began the process of planting the flower beds.

Over time the garden became a veritable extension of the museum, the site of events, classes, and exhibitions. With the creation of the café, and its expansion into the garden, the garden evolved further. In 2004, the museum began to host evening summer programs with live music as well.

As part of the most recent renovation, Baumann selected American landscape architect Walter Hood, the principal of Hood Design Studio, Oakland, California. Winner of the prestigious Cooper Hewitt National Design Award (2009), Hood has dedicated his career to public garden design. He has developed sensitive, community-inclusive landscapes across the country, including the M. H. de Young Museum in San Francisco, the Autry National Center in Los Angeles, and the Oakland Waterfront Center. For Cooper Hewitt, he activated all areas of the garden, even a western section traditionally used for storage.

In 2006 the museum opened the 90th Street garden entrance, providing greater access to the garden for the local neighborhood. This welcoming face was heightened with the addition in 2014 of a new canopy over the garden entrance, designed by Diller, Scofidio + Renfro. LED lights embedded in the corner pillars of the garden fence draw the eye to the museum campus. The new café, now more integrated into the outdoors than ever before, underscores how much the garden is a vital part of the museum.

A rendering of the Arthur Ross Terrace and Garden.

ACKNOWLEDGMENTS

I have many people to thank for their help with this project. I am grateful first of all to Laurel McEuen, who as a curatorial fellow during her M.A. studies at Cooper Hewitt worked tirelessly on this project and whose research on the origins of the museum collection, the relation of the Carnegies and the Cooper and Hewitt families, and the history of the mansion's organ is reflected in several sidebars in the book.

I would like to thank Cooper Hewitt curators Sarah Coffin and Gail Davidson for contributing essays on the Teak Room, Lockwood de Forest, and Carnegie's relationship with Tiffany—material that ultimately represented only a portion of the fascinating original research that they have been conducting on these subjects. Thank you to Henry Taves and Posy Bass for providing their Lockwood de Forest photograph. And to Kameleika Bose for her interpretation and research of the de Forest archive at the Archives of American Art.

I benefited greatly from the excellent earlier research on the history of the mansion done by Jacquelann Killian, former curatorial assistant at Cooper Hewitt; Andrew Dolkart, who produced the popular 2002 book on the mansion; and Amy Ballard, of the Smithsonian's office of Architectural History and Historic Preservation.

It's been a privilege to work with the exceptional staff at Cooper Hewitt—in particular: Director Caroline Baumann; Stephen Van Dyk; Matilda McQuaid; Cara McCarty; Janice Slivko; Sarah Coffin; Lucy Commoner; Seb Chan; Greg Herringshaw; Gail Davidson; Caitlin Condell; Nate Wilcox; Shamus Adams; Jen Northrop; Elizabeth Broman; Jennifer Cohlman Bracchi; Susan Brown; Kimberly Randall; Julie Barnes; Deborah Fitzgerald; Dontae Duran; Demian Cacciolo; Allison Hale; Ronald Peterson; Jesse Henderson. Above all, I've been very fortunate to have in Pamela Horn such an inspiring editor and project leader, and I cannot thank Matthew Kennedy enough for all the work he did to bring the book to publication.

Elsewhere at the Smithsonian I'm grateful to Sharon Park at Architectural History and Historic Preservation; Leslie Overstreet and Erin Rushing at Smithsonian Libraries; Charlotte Gaither of the Office of Advancement; Brandon Fortune, Ann Shumard, and Dorothy Moss at the National Portrait Gallery; Liza Kirwin and Wendy Hurlock Baker at the Archives of American Art; Lauryn Guttenplan and Farleigh Earhart in the office of the General Counsel; Kelly Crawford and William Donnelly at Smithsonian Gardens; Steven Turner, David Haberstich, Kay Peterson, Hal Wallace, and Peter Liebhold at the National Museum of American History; and, as ever, the entire staff of the Smithsonian Archives—especially Pamela Henson, Courtney Bellizzi, Tad Bennicoff, Ellen Alers, Tammy Peters, Marguerite Roby, Kira Cherrix, Nora Lockshin, Kirsten Tyree, and Michael Barnes.

In Pittsburgh, thanks to Greg Priore and Gilbert Pietrzak at the Carnegie Library of Pittsburgh; J. Dustin Williams, formerly of Carnegie Mellon University Archives, and Gabrielle Michalek, there now; and Holger Hoock.

In Scotland, thanks to Andrew Martindale of Historic Scotland; Simon Green of the Royal Commission on Ancient and Historic Monuments; Claire Bruce and Katy Renwick of the Carnegie Club at Skibo Castle; Lorna Owers of the Carnegie Birthplace Museum; Sue Higgins of the History Links Museum in Dornoch; Martin and Natalie Reid; and Liz McDonald at the Carnegie UK Trust.

Here in New York thanks to Gino Francesconi, archivist at Carnegie Hall, for sharing his passion for Carnegie history and his great knowledge of the family; Vartan Gregorian, Jeanne D'Onofrio, and Ron Sexton at Carnegie Corporation of New York; Jennifer Comins and Jocelyn Wilk at Columbia University Archives; Susan Henshaw Jones, Lindsay Turley, Grace Hernandez, Phyllis Magidson, and Nilda Riviera at the Museum of the City of New York; David Lowe, Stephen Pinson, Stephan Saks, and Thomas Lisanti at the New York Public Library; Janet Parks and Jason Escalante at Avery Drawings and Archives at Columbia University; Elizabeth Garnsey; Neepie and Billy Bourne; Matthew Worsnick; Margery Masinter; Carol Salomon and Mitsuko Brooks at Cooper Union Library; Marie Long at the New York Botanical Garden; Amy Aronofsky and Paul Schlotthauer at Pratt Institute Archive; and Taraneh Rohani of the Spence School.

I had fascinating conversations with a number of individuals who once worked for Cooper-Hewitt or were otherwise associated with the mansion: Cordelia Rose; Dorothy Globus; David McFadden; Mary Riley Smith; Lynden Miller; and Christa Thurman. I also benefited from conversations that others had, some as part of a Cooper-Hewitt oral history project, with Milton Sonday, Eugene Thaw, Elaine Evans Dee, and Janos Spitzer. Laurel

McEuen spoke to a number of alumni of the Columbia University School of Social Work, including Barbara Anderson, Laura Freund, Harriet Lubin, Barbara Solt, and Gaby Taub. Thanks to Jennifer March at Columbia for facilitating these contacts.

I am particularly grateful to Kenneth Miller for sharing his knowledge of his family history and his long experience as a board member of the museum, and for his careful and thoughtful read of the manuscript. Special thanks, too, to Linda Thorell Hills for sharing so much of what she knows of her family, including the volume of Margaret Carnegie's diaries she edited.

I'm grateful to the architects who shared with me their experiences of working on the mansion: Hugh Hardy; Timothy Hartung, Susan Strauss, and Michael Hassett of Ennead (formerly Polshek Partnership); Richard Southwick of Beyer Blinder Belle; and David Mayner and Richard Gluckman of Gluckman Mayner.

Thanks also to Marcelo Guidoli; Laurie Ossman; Mosette Broderick; Lee Gray; Shelley Bennett; Brian Daniels; Michael Kathrens; Umang Hutheesing; William Massa at Manuscripts & Archives, Yale University Library; Bruce Kirby at the Library of Congress; Maria Ketcham at the Detroit Institute of Arts; Carol Butler at Brown Brothers; Lauren Taylor; Dr. James Tucker; Elizabeth Doering; Patrick Amsellem; Frances Halsband; Daphne Williams Fox; Bannon McHenry; Parker Stephenson; William Crawford; Estella Chung and Vada Komistra at Hillwood; Christine Cordazzo at Esto; Lavinia Ciuffa at the American Academy in Rome; James Heustis Cook and Bynum Petty of the Organ Historical Society; Eisha Neely of the Division of Rare and Manuscript Collections at Cornell University; the staff of the Art, Architecture & Engineering Library at the University of Michigan; Katie Clark, Alana Zawojski Ippolito, and Nicolas Zurcher at IDEO; and Jennifer Keane and her mother Martha Hendrick Rusnak.

Kudos to Jimmy Rudnick for the beautiful contemporary photography, to Brankica Harvey, Yo-E Ryou, and Eddie Opara at Pentagram for the floorplans and map, and to Diller Scofidio + Renfro and Thinc Design for their renderings. Tremendous thanks to Miko McGinty, Rita Jules, and Anjali Pala for creating such a wonderful design for the book, and to Eileen Chetti for the excellent copyediting. And thank you to Furthermore: a program of the J. M. Kaplan Fund for its generous support.

PHOTO CREDITS

Published by:
Cooper Hewitt, Smithsonian Design Museum
2 East 91st Street
New York, NY 10128
USA
cooperhewitt.org

Distributed Worldwide by ARTBOOK | D.A.P.
155 Sixth Avenue, 2nd floor
New York, NY 10013
USA
artbook.com

Library of Congress
Cataloging-in-Publication Data

Ewing, Heather P.
  Life of a mansion : the story of Cooper
Hewitt, Smithsonian Design Museum /
Heather Ewing.
    p. cm.
  Includes index.
  ISBN 978-0-910503-71-6
1. Cooper-Hewitt Museum—History. 2.
Carnegie, Andrew, 1835–1919—Homes and
haunts—New York (State)—New York. 3. New
York (N.Y.)—Buildings, structures, etc. I.
Cooper-Hewitt Museum. II. Title.

  NK460.N4C664 2014
745.4074'7471--dc23

2014020723

ISBN: 978-0-910503-71-6 (flexi-bound)
ISBN: 978-0-910503-72-3 (epub)
ISBN: 978-0-910503-73-0 (.mobi)

Pamela Horn
Head of Cross-Platform Publishing
Cooper Hewitt, Smithsonian Design Museum

Design: Miko McGinty and Rita Jules
Cooper Hewitt branding and logo design:
  Eddie Opara, Pentagram
Fonts: Galaxie Polaris and Cooper Hewitt
  designed by Chester Jenkins

On the front cover: Grand staircase with
  Caldwell chandelier; photo by Andrew Garn
  © Smithsonian Institution.
On the back cover: Southeast view of Carnegie
  Mansion and Garden; photo by Elizabeth
  Felicella © Smithsonian Institution.
On the front endpaper: Grand staircase with
  Caldwell chandelier; photo by Andrew Garn
  © Smithsonian Institution.
On the back endpaper: Carved oak detail; photo
  by James Rudnick.
On page 2: Detail of the decorative plasterwork
  in the Drawing Room ceiling; photo by
  James Rudnick.
On page 4: Detail of one of the decorative stone
  urn finials atop the roof parapet; photo by
  James Rudnick.

2014 2015 2016 2017 / 10 9 8 7 6 5 4 3 2 1

PRINTED IN CHINA

Furthermore:
a program of the J.M. Kaplan Fund